Mushrooms
of the Boreal Forest

Eugene F. Bossenmaier

UNIVERSITY EXTENSION PRESS
UNIVERSITY OF SASKATCHEWAN

If you eat mushrooms you find, you are doing so at your own risk. While every effort has been made to ensure that the information contained in this publication is correct, the author and publisher caution against the use of the information in any particular application and accept no responsibility or liability for errors, omissions or representations, expressed or implied, contained herein. Neither the author nor the publisher accept responsibility or liability for errors the reader might make in identifying mushrooms, for harmful reactions to eating poisonous mushrooms, or for idiosyncratic reactions to eating any mushrooms.

Printed in Canada.

07   06   05   04   5   4   3

Canadian Cataloguing in Publication Data

Bossenmaier, Eugene F., 1924–1999

Mushrooms of the boreal forest

ISBN 0-88880-355-9

1. Mushrooms – Boreal Forest – Saskatchewan – Identification. I. Title.

QK617.B67 1997   579.6'097124'2   C97–920039–3

Published by University Extension Press, University of Saskatchewan

Readers with questions or comments or who would like to examine specimens of mushrooms mentioned in this book are invited to contact the author through the publisher.

For other questions or additional copies, please contact University Extension Press, University of Saskatchewan, Rm #125–117 Science Place, Saskatoon, SK, Canada, S7N 5C8 ph: (306) 966-5565; e-mail: uep.books@usask.ca; www.uep.usask.ca

Photography: Eugene F. Bossenmaier, except 54A by Gerry Ivanochko

Cover photo appearance: Thank you to Sandra Martens

University Extension Press
University of Saskatchewan

Project Co-ordinator and Editor: Peter Jonker

Layout and Cover Design: Stan Ruecker

Support: Sandra Cey & Allison Muri

Illustrations: Michael Misanchuk

Dedication

To my grandchildren who, on outing after outing, proved the old adage:
kids find more mushrooms.

A NOTE OF CAUTION. . .

Picking mushrooms in the boreal forest region of Saskatchewan is generally permitted except in Prince Albert National Park. Anyone who intends to gather wild mushrooms for the table should heed the following warning:

**Never eat a mushroom unless you are absolutely sure of its identity
and have checked reliable sources as to its edibility.**

There are mushrooms in the boreal forest that, if eaten, can cause sickness and others that can cause death. Some safe mushrooms have deadly look-alikes; an error in identification can be fatal.

Getting lost in the forest is another danger facing mushroomers. Solution:

Always carry a map and compass and know how to use them.

From personal experience of being lost in the park, I always carry a compass now, even on sunny days when I plan to stay on mapped trails. Should the sun cloud over and you leave the trail even for short distances with your head down in search of mushrooms, it is almost certain you will be disoriented when you look up and search for your direction back to the trail. At a moment like this a compass can be your most valuable possession. Being lost in a vast forest is a terrifying experience—don't chance it!

Bears are another concern. Before going into the field it is advisable to **bring yourself up to date on bear signs, how to avoid bear encounters, and how to conduct yourself most safely in an encounter.**

Most parks and natural resource departments publish relevant information.

Contents

Financial Contributors

This publication has been made possible through generous donations from:

Saskfor MacMillan
Limited Partnership

Parks Canada
Prince Albert National Park

Weyerhaeuser Canada

Saskatchewan Division

MISTIK
MANAGEMENT LTD.

Industry Canada   Industrie Canada

L & M Wood Products

Shell Environmental Fund

Saskatchewan
Heritage
FOUNDATION

Agriculture and
Agri-Food Canada

Prairie Farm Rehabilitation
Administration

Agriculture et
Agroalimentaire Canada

Administration du rétablissement
agricole des Prairies

Preface

My first view of Prince Albert National Park was back in July 1950 from a low-flying aircraft carrying several waterfowl biologists and students to the park village of Waskesiu Lake to attend a conference on the prairie duck situation. We were advised to look for moose; this park we were told could not boast of snow-capped mountains or wild rivers. What we saw was a vast tract of rolling, heavily forested country featuring, toward the north, several large wilderness lakes. Little did I realize at the time that wild mushrooms were an important component of the park and that 40 years later I would be walking in the forest below identifying species and enjoying their beauty and diversity.

My interest in mushrooms arose from my work as a wildlife biologist in Manitoba. Mushrooms were common members of many wildlife habitats but, although they caught our attention, they were mostly overlooked on our surveys because their biology and life histories were little understood and their identities unknown. It was not until I had spent several enjoyable days in the field with Mike Klywak that the world of mushrooms began to unfold for me. Mike emigrated to Canada from Ukraine in 1928 and spent most of the ensuing years cutting saw logs, pulp wood, firewood and Christmas trees in and around Agassiz Provincial Forest east of Winnipeg. He didn't know any scientific names but he could recognize many mushroom species, knew when and where to find them, and was a master chef in preparing them for the table. My family and I soon caught his enthusiasm for wild mushrooms.

When my wife and I moved to a farm near the southern edge of Prince Albert National Park in 1988, we were intent on becoming acquainted with the mushrooms of the area. It was disappointing to learn on our arrival that there was so little known of these organisms in the park, or in Saskatchewan for that matter. Where to start?

The Cuelenaere Library in Prince Albert introduced me to an excellent guide, David Arora's 1986 book, *Mushrooms Demystified*. My interest was further nurtured by attending Arora's U.S. Thanksgiving weekend mushroom class at Albion, California, in 1991. While passing through the Calgary Air Terminal on this trip, I discovered a newly published book, *Mushrooms of Western Canada*, by Helene M.E. Schalkwijk-Barendsen. The preliminaries for my intensive study of the mushrooms of Prince Albert National Park and vicinity were now complete. Field work over the next five summers—1992 to 1996—produced the observations and photographs that are recorded in this book.

I am indebted to Peter Jonker and Bertram Wolfe for their initial encouragement, and to them and others with the Extension Division, University of Saskatchewan, for carrying this book through to completion. I am also grateful to members of the park staff—Merv Syroteuk, Marilyn and Doug Anions, Lisa Chevalier, Susan Carr, Brad Muir, Adam Pidwerbeski, Michael Fitzsimmons, Dave Dalman, Murray Heap—for permits and other services; to Scott Redhead, Randy Currah (and associates), Yasu Hiratsuka and Leni and

John Schalkwijk, experts in the field, for advice freely given; to Kalya Brunner, Len Donais and Dorothy Bird, mushroom enthusiasts, for information on local species; to staff of the Cuelenaere Library, Prince Albert, for graciously acting on my many requests; to Gerry Ivanochko, with the Saskatchewan Government in La Ronge, for information on mushrooms in the north of the province; to Carla Zelmer, leader of a fungus research study in the park, for being available whenever I needed assistance or mycological expertise; to the people of the Mayview district who welcomed us into their midst and aided the study in numerous ways; to my wife, Alice, who, in addition to putting up with mushroom mania for several summers, provided unstinting support toward both the photography and the text; to Mary Jean, Steven and Greta who encouraged their dad from start to finish. Much of the credit for this book belongs to these people; all the weaknesses and errors are mine.

Many thanks also to the several agencies, identified on page vi, whose generous financial contributions made this production possible.

About This Book

This book highlights distinctive groups and species of boreal forest mushrooms that were identified and photographed in Saskatchewan's Prince Albert National Park (PANP) and vicinity. It is meant for the person who would like to enter the fascinating world of mushrooms without having to resort to the use of technical literature or a microscope and chemicals.

Mushroom identification in the field taxes even the advanced student, so a beginner should not expect any field guide to make the job swift and simple. Guides to birds, mammals, trees and wildflowers may be complete and relatively easy to use; popular guides to mushrooms are never complete and therefore often fall short of expectations. There are just too many species of mushrooms that, because of their close outward resemblance to other species, require laboratory examination for accurate identification. Field guides for general use emphasize the more distinctive species; they screen out a multitude of difficult kinds. A novice mushroomer should not become dismayed when she or he encounters specimens that cannot be identified with the book or books at hand—it is all part of the game.

Identification is only one aspect of mushrooming; curiosity of people on field trips always extends to questions dealing with the biology of mushrooms, their roles in forest ecosystems and, of course, their fitness for the kitchen. Short discussions on these topics are included in this book.

A glossary and an index are provided in the back. Look in the glossary for definitions of technical and other terms used in the text. The index lists, by page numbers, the scientific and common names of mushrooms and items of general interest found in the book.

Finally, throughout the rather structured format of this guidebook, you will find a healthy sprinkling of mushroom lore, facts and trivia.

Source: Canadian Council on Ecological Areas, 1996. *A Perspective on Canada's Ecosystems.*

Prince Albert National Park

The Boreal Forest

The boreal or great northern forest covers a wide expanse of Canada from the Atlantic Ocean to the Rocky Mountains, extending in places into the United States. Most Canadians know it as the land of white spruce, jack pine, poplar and balsam fir, spotted with stands of white birch and bogs of black spruce and tamarack. Not so well known is that the boreal forest also extends across northern Europe and Asia.

None of the fungi described and illustrated in this book is found exclusively in the boreal forest of Saskatchewan. All have much wider distribution. A few are known only regionally, such as in eastern or western North America. Most, however, are found across all of North America. Furthermore, many are circumboreal (around the entire Northern Hemisphere). Thus, many of the mushrooms in this book are encountered not only in Canada and the United States but also in Europe and Asia.

Using This Book for Your Learning

Enter a forest after midsummer rains and you will be met by a profusion of mushrooms, possibly in overawing quantity and diversity. But in that sea of mushrooms are some that stand out for some reason or another, like green-headed male mallards in a flock of mixed ducks. More than 200 species of distinctive mushrooms of the boreal forest are highlighted in this book. Start your venture into the world of forest mushrooms by learning some of these "easy" ones; you can always graduate to more difficult ones later.

A first step is to become familiar with the organization of the descriptions and photographs in this book. You will note that the mushrooms are arranged by major groups—Gilled, Ridged, Fleshy Pored, Toothed, etc.—and then by families, genera, and species within the major groups. Each species is referenced by its page number followed by its letter; thus 6B refers to page six, item B. On the left page of each two-page spread you will find a brief description of the species' important characteristics; on the right page, its corresponding photograph.

When in the field, take a particular mushroom in hand, examine it, and place it in the proper major group. Then try to match it with one of the species in this book. You may be lucky and come up with a perfect match on the first try. More likely, however, especially if you picked a gilled mushroom, your early attempts at identification will leave you less than completely satisfied. If it is any consolation, even experts are puzzled by some of the mushrooms they find on outings.

Although arriving at the exact species of many gilled mushrooms may prove to be impossible, much satisfaction can come from being able to say a troublesome specimen belongs to this or that family or genus. Become familiar with families and genera that have prominent characteristics. This will enable you to more precisely classify many mushrooms, even though their exact names will remain a mystery. Key features of many families and genera are included in this book.

Some readers may want to accept the challenge of probing deeper into the complexities of mushroom identification. This can be done in two stages: an intermediate stage, that employs spore prints and detailed keys—like those found in Arora (1986)—and an advanced stage, that calls for technical literature, microscopic examination and chemical testing. (Recently, DNA analysis has come into use.) Information on these methods and techniques is available from most public libraries.

For those interested in additional information on the families, genera, and species contained in this book, relevant page numbers from five more broadly based field guides are provided (in brackets) at the end of each description. For example, (A 231) refers you to Arora, David, page 231. These books were my basic references. The five are the following:

Arora, David. 1986, *Mushrooms Demystified,* Second Edition, Ten Speed Press, Berkeley.

Groves, J. Walton. 1979, *Edible and Poisonous Mushrooms of Canada,* Research Branch, Agriculture Canada, Publication 1112, Ottawa.

Lincoff, Gary H. 1981, *The Audubon Society Field Guide to North American Mushrooms*, Alfred A. Knopf, New York.

McKnight, Kent H. and Vera B. 1987, *A Field Guide to Mushrooms— North America*, Peterson Field Guide Series #34, Houghton Mifflin Company, Boston.

Schalkwijk-Barendsen, Helene M.E. 1991, *Mushrooms of Western Canada,* Lone Pine Publishing, Edmonton.

Spore Colour and Spore Prints

An examination of any of the above books reveals major emphasis on the colour of the spores in the identification process for gilled mushrooms, and to a lesser degree for the fleshy-pored group. Spore colour, except in a few instances, is not emphasized in this book because it introduces another complication and is not needed for recognizing the truly distinctive species. Determining spore colour, however, can be both interesting and informative; it helps to confirm identifications and is a step toward naming more difficult specimens. Often enough, the spore colour of a white-gilled mushroom comes as a surprise. If you do nothing more than experiment with a few caps, you will be rewarded with some striking colours and patterns. Spore prints should always be made and examined when a new species is being considered as possibly edible.

The process of arriving at spore colour by making a spore print is quite simple. Start by collecting firm, mature specimens and bringing them home separately in small paper bags or wrapped in waxed paper (not plastic bags or wraps, which hasten deterioration). At home, cut off the stalk flush with the bottom of the cap and place the cap, gills or pores down, on a piece of white paper. Cover the cap with a bowl or plastic dairy container and leave for a few hours or overnight. The result is a print made up of thousands of microscopic spores (See illustration 6B for an example). White spore prints become clearer when viewed at an angle. Now view the spores through a microscope, if one is available, to get an idea of the characteristics—in addition to colour—used by advanced students for identifying more difficult species.

Biology, Ecology and Anatomy of Mushrooms

Some Basic Biology

Mushrooms are the fruiting bodies of fungi. Fungi comprise their own kingdom of living organisms comparable to the animal and plant kingdoms. The fungi highlighted in this book form only a small part of the fungal kingdom, which also includes yeasts and molds.

The primary function of mushrooms is to cast spores for new generations of fungi. Mushrooms are sent out by the vegetative portion of the fungus called the mycelium, a network of cellular filaments or threads that permeate trees, logs, stumps, needles, leaves, moss, humus and other kinds of forest organic matter. The mycelium, of course, is buried and out of sight but can often be made visible by examining the organic matter under the base of the mushroom where the whitish mycelium appears as threads or a cottony mat. It is extremely difficult to inventory and study the fungal component of forest communities. The vegetative portion is hidden and mostly unrecognizable as to species, while mushroom production itself is too erratic to be used as an accurate indicator of the presence, distribution and abundance of many fungi in the forest.

Fungi exist through the absorption of nutrients by the mycelium. If a particular fungus absorbs nutrients from dead organic matter, it is said to be saprophytic (Greek: decaying vegetation); if it absorbs nutrients from living organisms, such as a tree, it is said to be parasitic; if it absorbs nutrients from the roots of living vegetation and reciprocates in some beneficial manner, it is said to be mycorrhizal (Greek: fungus root). All three kinds of fungi are common in the northern forest and all produce showy mushrooms.

Some Basic Ecology

Forest ecosystems depend on fungi for their survival. Saprophytic species of fungi, through the secretion of enzymes, decompose enormous amounts of dead organic materials and, aided by bacteria, free inorganic nutrients for recycling through new forest growth. Parasitic species appeared to be of minor significance on my study areas. Their exact roles in the forest ecosystem were not clear. Mycorrhizal species, through a fusion of their mycelia with the roots of living trees, exchange nutrients with their hosts: the trees receive essential minerals, trace elements and water, and the fungi receive food (carbohydrates), which the trees produce through photosynthesis. Thriving trees and their mushroom partners are a reflection of this mutually beneficial relationship.

It is not always easy to classify a species of fungi as saprophytic or mycorrhizal; the mushroom by itself does not reveal the fungus' mode of existence. However, if the mushrooms are growing from rotten stumps or logs, or are attached to fallen leaves or needles, the species can be assumed to be saprophytic. If a species forms a large group on sand under jack pine, it is probably mycorrhizal. Other growth situations, such as on humus or moss, can be more difficult to interpret. Researchers have established the modes of existence for most fungi and these are mentioned under the descriptions of mushrooms in this book.

Mushrooms are important components of food webs in forest ecosystems. In addition to spreading spores, mushrooms feed numerous animals, such as deer and squirrels, and harbour the larval stages of a myriad of insects. One can't help but wonder about the complex interrelationships that must exist among mushrooms, insects and birds in the forest.

Some Basic Anatomy

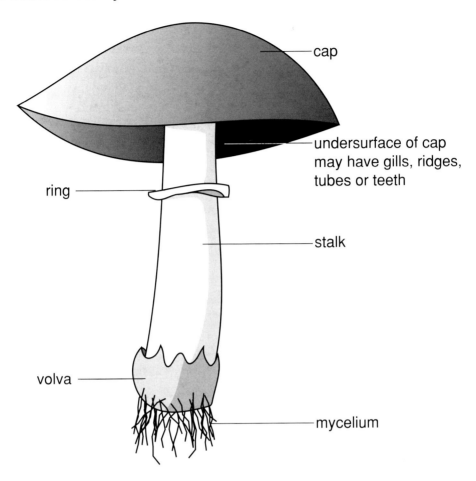

The presence or absence of a ring or a volva, and variations in size, shape, colour, texture, surface features and so forth of the several parts, help to distinguish families, genera and species of fungi.

Appreciating Forest Ecosystems Through Fungi

An added bonus to mushrooming is the familiarity that one develops with the forest as a whole and with its many different communities. To see a reasonable cross section of forest mushrooms it is necessary to visit every kind of forest habitat several times during the season of mushroom production, which usually extends from early May to early October. (During winter months, when hiking or on cross-country skis or snowshoes, you have a good opportunity to become familiar with mushrooms that overwinter on standing trees). One soon becomes acquainted with young and old, pure and mixed stands of white spruce (*Picea glauca*), poplar (both white, *Populus tremuloides*, and black or balsam, *P. balsamifera*), jack pine (*Pinus banksiana*), balsam fir (*Abies balsamea*), white birch (*Betula papyrifera*), black spruce (*Picea mariana*) and tamarack (*Larix laricina*).

Thorough coverage of different forest habitats is required because every kind and variety of forest organic matter can be, and probably is, home to one or more species of saprophytic fungi. And, every kind of tree may have mycorrhizal fungal partners. Many species of fungi are substrate- or tree-specific and seasonal; that is, their mushrooms are found only on a particular kind of organic matter, such as rotting spruce stumps or logs, or only in association with a particular kind of tree, and then for only a short period of time, say early spring or late summer. After a field trip or two, new mushroomers have been heard to exclaim: "So many different habitats! So many different substrates! So many different mushrooms!"

Two of the most revealing times to go mushrooming are during and after summer rains. Several species that shrivel up during dry spells expand and become much more conspicuous when wet. Other species become viscid and glisten in the rain. Some small, fragile mushrooms are ephemeral and may be missed entirely if not spotted during or shortly after rainy periods. I always find the forest to be especially inviting when it is still dripping wet.

A few days after heavy rains the forest floor becomes a sea of larger, more robust mushrooms. This is the time to fully appreciate the extent to which fungi permeate forest ecosystems. One might be inclined to minimize the abundance of fungi, and therefore their significance, when mushrooms are virtually non-existent following a month of summer drought. But their true place in the forest world is made evident when their fruiting bodies appear virtually everywhere. Many happenings in forest ecosystems are mysterious, the greatest in my estimation being life beneath the forest floor. A major flush of mushrooms in the forest can be an impressive indicator of, and a window on, these hidden activities.

Mushrooming inevitably increases one's appreciation for other forest phenomena. A mushroomer, moving along at an unhurried pace, will meet many resident birds and mammals. In time, one may encounter, among other things, a cow moose and her calf feeding at the edge of a forest pond, timber wolves crossing the trail ahead, curious black bears, newly hatched broods of ruffed and spruce grouse, inquisitive great grey owls and territorial goshawks. Studying fungi is seen by some people as an unparalleled opportunity for getting to know and keeping in touch with forest ecosystems.

SPECIES
DESCRIPTIONS
AND
PHOTOGRAPHS

Gilled Fungi
(Undersurfaces of caps have gills)

Note the ring on the stalk. The ring is the remains of a veil that extends from the edge of the cap to the stalk on some young mushrooms. The absence or presence of a ring and its peculiarities help to distinguish species. Also useful are such physical attributes as whether the gills are free from or attached to the stalk and the manner of attachment.

Family Agaricaceae

Agaricus is the sole genus placed here. Its main claim to fame is that it contains the well-known cultivated mushroom. Discover the characteristics of this large genus by examining the common white mushroom in the produce section of your food store.

Genus *Agaricus*

Three woodland species are illustrated. Other less distinctive species occur but can be identified to genus by their free gills (not attached to the stalk); gills that are white when young, then turning pink and finally browning with age; dark brown spore print and a veil that leaves a ring on the stalk. Members of the genus are terrestrial and saprophytic. (A 310; G 200; L 500; M 254; S 325)

Agaricus haemorrhoidarius   Bleeding Agaricus
Brownish, fibrous-scaly cap; bruised flesh quickly turns an unexpected red. Not common or widespread. One dependable site was an area of moist moss under black spruce in late summer. Edible but not recommended because of possible misidentification. A similar brown, scaly-capped Agaricus with flesh that does not bruise red occurs in same habitats as *A. silvicola* and may be a variant of *A. silvicola* (Schalkwijk-Barendsen 330).
(A 325; G 202; L 505; M 258; S 327)

A

Agaricus semotus   Wine Agaricus
Small and delicate with pinkish colouration on a yellowish cap. Note the free gills, ring and gill colour. Odour strongly aromatic of almond. During summer in leaf and needle duff under white spruce. Common only two summers during study. Edible but small size discourages picking.
(A 340; G 201; S 328)

B

Agaricus silvicola   Woodland Agaricus
A white Agaricus that sometimes shows touches of yellow when bruised; crushed flesh has mild almond odour. There is a resemblance to the deadly *Amanita virosa*, but *Amanita virosa* has gills that stay white and a sac-like cup (volva) at the base of the stalk. *Agaricus silvicola* occurs all summer on the ground under spruce and poplar. Edible but not recommended because of resemblance to poisonous species.
(A 334; G 203; L 501; M 261; S 330)

C1

Same species as C1. A young specimen; cap still round and unexpanded; veil between cap edge and stalk still complete; gills white but beginning to show pink. Always uncover base of stalk; if there is a membranous cup sheathing the base, the mushroom is probably the deadly poisonous *Amanita virosa*.

C2

Mushroom Poisoning

Entire books have been written about the poisons found in wild mushrooms. The subject need not be fearsome for people who know their edible species. What makes it fascinating are the wide variety of these poisons and their differing effects on the human body. A common classification of mushroom poisoning includes the following:

- slow acting cellular poisons that often lead to kidney and liver failure and death;
- a poison that interacts with alcohol in the body to produce painful but passing effects;
- stomach and digestive system poisons;
- nervous system poisons;
- hallucinogens.

(For further reading: *Poisonous Mushrooms of Canada*. 1985. Joseph F. Ammirati et. al. Research Branch, Agriculture Canada, Monograph 30.)

Gilled Fungi

A

B

C1

C2

Family Amanitaceae

There are two genera: *Amanita* and *Limacella*. Gills are white and free from (not attached to) the stalk. Spore print is white.
(A 262; L 525; M 213; S 226)

Genus *Amanita*   The Amanitas

Only the three illustrated species were encountered. Another member of this genus, *Amanita virosa* (The Destroying Angel), an extremely poisonous species, has been reported from Alberta and may occur in Prince Albert National Park. A distinguishing feature of this genus is the egg-shaped body (see photos 5A and 5B1) from which the cap and stalk emerge, leaving a membranous sack or scaly bulb—the volva—at the base of the stalk (that is sometimes partially or completely buried). Members are
(A 263; G 77; L 525; M 215; S 226)   mycorrhizal.

Amanita fulva   Tawny Grisette
Handsome, tan coloured with a large membranous cup around base of stalk; margin of cap striate (grooved). It closely resembles the grey-coloured *Amanita vaginata* with which it is sometimes found. Appears during summer under poplar and birch. Reported as edible but not recommended because of deadly close kin. (See also photo on p. 23)
        (A 287; G 93; L 536; M 238; S 229)

A

Amanita muscaria   Fly Amanita
Yellow to orange caps ornamented with white flakes. The basal bulb has scaly rings rather than a membranous sack. The Fly Amanita is very striking when found in large groups from "eggs" to platter-sized specimens. A vertical cross section through an Amanita "egg" reveals the preformed mushroom. On the forest floor under poplar and white spruce in summer and fall. Poisonous.
        (A 282; G 83; L 540; M 227; S 227)

B1

Same species as B1. An expanded cap; some grow so large they topple over. Probably the most illustrated wild mushroom. Said to be the species nibbled on by Alice in Lewis Carroll's *Adventures in Wonderland*. Contains a toxic substance that stuns flies—hence the common name.

B2

Amanita vaginata   Grisette
Tall, grey and stately with a loose basal membrane. Cap sometimes decorated with membranous fragments; margin of cap strongly grooved. Scattered under poplar along trails and in open forest during summer. Reported edible but not recommended because of deadly close kin.
(A 288; G 93; L 549; M 237; S 228)

C

Genus *Limacella*

Limacella glioderma   Fox-Coloured Limacella
A striking mushroom at its prime; reddish-brown, sticky cap with reddish-brown scales on stalk below a wispy ring. Summer and fall under spruce and poplar; saprophytic. Edibility unknown.
(A 291; G 94; L 554; M 214; S 230)

D

Limacella illinita   White Limacella
Easy to distinguish at the stage when it is snow white and covered with slime. A yellowish form also occurs. It has free gills, i.e., they are not attached to the stalk. Late summer under jack pine, spruce and poplar. Never common during study. Saprophytic. Edibility unknown. Resembles two species of snow-white, viscid waxy caps discussed later but *Limacella illinita* has non-waxy, free gills.
        (A 292; G 94; M 214; S 230)

E

Folklore held that mushrooms are loathsome and should be avoided by children, along with snakes, toads, bats and spiders. (Enlightenment has softened this view but it is wise to teach children to be suspicious of mushrooms because the childhood habit of nibbling on things in the outdoors could have unpleasant results if the "things" turn out to be toxic mushrooms.)

A

B1

B2

C

D

E

Gilled Fungi

Family Bolbitiaceae

Two species that stand out in this family of mostly plain mushrooms are featured.
(A 466; L 555; M 304; S 312)

Genus *Agrocybe*
(A 467; L 555; M 304; S 313)

Agrocybe acericola   Stump Agrocybe
A mature specimen; yellowish brown in colour; gills dull brown; ring on stalk that becomes brownish with spores. May appear early in spring. Saprophytic, found on rotted poplar; not terrestrial as *A. praecox*. Not recommended for the table—can be confused with poisonous species.
(A 470; G 185; L 556; M 304; S 314)

A

Agrocybe praecox   Spring Agrocybe
A cream-coloured to brownish mushroom. Occurrence in early spring, the veil between the cap edge and stalk and the gills attached to the stalk help to distinguish this species. Terrestrial in open poplar and grassy areas; saprophytic. It is shown with its brown spore print. Edible but not recommended because of possible confusion with other species.
(A 469; G 185; L 558; M 305; S 313)

B

Family Coprinaceae

Distinctive species from two genera are shown: *Coprinus* and *Psathyrella*.
(A 341; L 596; M 276; S 331)

Genus *Coprinus*   The Inky Caps

Three distinct and one unidentified species are illustrated from a large genus. Some species are small, indistinct, and ephemeral. Properties of the genus include black spores and autodigestion, which turns the gills into inky fluid. Saprophytic.
(A 342; G 209; L 596; M 276; S 331)

Coprinus atramentarius   Inky Cap
Greyish, bell-shaped caps with whitish gills that turn black and inky. Sometimes in large clusters at the base of poplar stumps and trunks. Also known as "alcohol inky" after its tendency to produce physical discomfort and possibly nausea when consumed with alcoholic beverages. Found summer into fall. Edible but avoid with alcoholic drink.
   (A 347; G 211; L 596; M 276; S 335)

C

Coprinus comatus   Shaggy Mane
Also known as Lawyer's Wig. Easily recognized: tall and cylindrical; white with brown crown and shaggy, brown-tipped scales; gradually turning black and inky. Along roads and trails under mixed forest; most Augusts and Septembers. Edible and popular.
(A 345; G 211; L 597; M 277; S 332)

D

Old wives' tales are still recited in answer to questions on mushroom edibility. The truth is that
- dangerous ones do *not* always look distasteful;
- mushrooms that smell and taste good are *not* necessarily safe to eat;
- some deadly ones do *not* darken silver;
- if it peels it is *not* always good to eat.

A

B

In addition:
- some species eaten by forest animals (deer, mice, squirrels, insects, maggots) are *not* safe for human consumption.

Read the section on mushroom edibility, p. 92, before eating any wild mushroom.

C

D

Gilled Fungi

Coprinus micaceus   Glistening Inky Cap
Tan, striated, granular-coated caps, granules disappearing. Has less tendency to turn into an inky mass at maturity. Usually under poplar in dense clumps on wood, which may be buried. Fruits in summer and fall. Edible.
(A 348; G 212; L 600; M 278; S 334)

A

Coprinus sp.
Greyish, striated cap; margin curling inwards in age and turning inky; fragile. Following rains in leaf litter under poplar; ephemeral. One of several species of *Coprinus* with a life span measured in hours rather than days. Species uncertain; edibility unknown.

B

Genus *Psathyrella*   The Psathyrellas

A genus worth knowing because it is encountered frequently in poplar stands starting in early spring. Many members, however, are dull in appearance and difficult to identify. One unusual feature common to several species is the striking change in colour, from dark to light, that occurs as the caps lose moisture (these species are therefore said to be hygrophanous). Psathyrellas have grey to blackish gills and dark brown to purple-brown to blackish spores; many are found in clusters on decaying wood and at the base of poplars; saprophytic.
(A 361; G 208; L 596; M 281; S 337)

Psathyrella hydrophila   Clustered Psathyrella
Species in doubt; outward features that set this species apart from similar Psathyrellas are not pronounced. Cap dark brown at first, fading to tan; flimsy veil leaves remnants on cap edge. In clusters on poplar logs and stumps; early spring and beyond. Edibility unknown.
(A 364; G 208; L 607; M 283; S 339)

C

Psathyrella spadicea Date-Coloured Psathyrella
Questionable identity at level of species; can be confused with other members of genus. Cap date-coloured fading to tan; no veil between cap edge and stalk. In clumps on poplar stumps and at base of live, old poplars; summer. Edibility unknown.
(A 364; L 605; S 339)

D

Psathyrella uliginicola   Bog Psathyrella
Not as distinctive as most species in this book but the silky, grey, grooved cap is diagnostic. Gills are off-white to greyish. Spore colour comes as a surprise: dark purplish brown. It is not hygrophanous. Found all summer dispersed under poplar and white spruce. Edibility unknown.
(A 362; M 284; S 339)

E

Anemone patens (pasque-flower) blooms under jack pine in early May when snow drifts are still present in forest. This flower heralds the arrival of spring along with earliest mushrooms, notably *Mycena overholtzii* (Snowbank Fairy Helmet), 48C.

A

B

Prior to the microscope and the discovery of spores, mushrooms had no apparent method of reproduction (no visible seeds, so to speak). It was noted, however, that they erupted in the wake of summer storms. Folklore claimed they were a product of spontaneous generation set off by lightning and thunder.

Gilled Fungi

C

D

E

Family Cortinariaceae

A large, brown-spored family of several important genera.
(A 396; L 610; M 287; S 291)

Genus *Cortinarius*   The Corts

There are probably more species of *Cortinarius* in Prince Albert National Park and vicinity than any other genus of fungi. It is a frustrating group because many members are attractive and abundant but cannot be easily or reliably identified by field characters alone. Fortunately, the genus itself can be recognized by the presence of a cortina—a silky veil that extends from the cap to the stalk, especially noticeable on young specimens. As the mushroom matures the cortina collapses on the stalk where it catches brown spores, which are characteristic of the genus. The corts are mycorrhizal and appear in most habitats.
(A 417; G 179; L 610; M 287; S 291)

Genus *Cortinarius*
Showing the cortina that is characteristic of the genus. The cortina is not always this conspicuous. It soon collapses, leaving only wispy traces on the stalk.

A

Cortinarius alboviolaceus   Silvery-Violet Cortinarius
Cap and stalk silvery violet; stalk often dusted with brown spores. Note brown spores on stalk of right mushroom and cortina on central specimen. Scattered or grouped in humus under mixed white spruce and poplar; late summer. Edible with caution because of possible confusion with other species.
(A 447; G 180; L 611; S 299)

B

Cortinarius cinnamomeus   Yellow Cortinarius
Tawny-coloured cap; yellow gills. This is one of several closely related and similar appearing species that have vividly coloured gills. Most Yellow Cortinarius were recorded in feather moss under jack pine in late summer. Not recommended for eating.
(A 453; G 182; L 615)

C

Cortinarius semisanguineus   Eastern Red-Dye
Yellow-brown cap; blood-red gills; closely related to previous species, *C. cinnamomeus*. In moss under jack pine and spruce; late summer. Not recommended for eating.
(A 454; G 182; L 618; M 293; S 298)

D

Cortinarius trivialis   Early Cortinarius
Slimy coating and banded stalk are characteristic. If "trivialis" is taken to mean "commonplace," this species is well named. Some years everywhere in leaf litter under poplar from early spring to midsummer. Reported as edible but not recommended because of risky close relatives.
(A 431; M 289; S 293)

E

Cortinarius violaceus   Purple Cortinarius
An outstanding species in a difficult genus. Brown spores adhering to the collapsed cortina on the deep blue stalk confirm its identity. If there is adequate moisture in midsummer, look for this uncommon species in moss beds in old-growth white spruce stands. Original description of the genus *Cortinarius* was based on this species. Reported as edible but of poor quality.
(A 446; G 182; L 620; M 294; S 299)

F

Sac and Club Fungi

Mycologists separate the species of fungi found in popular field guides into two major groups, the Ascomycetes or "sac fungi" and the Basidiomycetes or "club fungi." In sac fungi the spores develop inside specialized sac-like cells (asci); in club fungi they develop on specialized club-shaped cells (basidia). The morels, false morels, elfin saddles and cup fungi are the better known sac fungi. Most other popular mushrooms are club fungi.

A

B

C

D

E

F

Gilled Fungi

Genus *Crepidotus*

Occupants of decomposing wood. Sometimes difficult to arrive at actual species—there are several in the area—but all have brown spores, are fan- or kidney-shaped and are mostly stalkless. The gills radiate fan-like from a more or less common point on the base of the cap.
(A 405; G 198; L 636; M 295; S 306)

Crepidotus applanatus   Flat Crepidotus
Questionable identity at level of species; open to confusion with other members of genus. White, shell-shaped caps, often dusted with cinnamon-brown spores. In overlapping clusters on decomposed poplar logs; summer. Edibility unknown.
(A 406; G 198; L 636; M 295; S 307)

A

Credipotus cinnabarinus   Red Crepidotus
The small, red caps stand out against the dark, rotting poplar log. The gills too are reddish. Midsummer; not common. Edibility unknown.
(A 405; G 198; M 296; S 307)

B

Crepidotus mollis   Soft Crepidotus
Yellowish-brown caps covered with hairy scales; older caps may be smooth and flabby. Common; found on decaying poplar logs and branches during summer. Edibility unknown.
(A 406; G 198; L 637; M 295; S 308)

C

Genus *Galerina*

Home to many "little brown mushrooms" (LBMs; see p.17). Avoid confusion with similar appearing Mycenas by checking spore prints: *Galerina*, brown; *Mycena*, white.
(A 399; G 188; M 296; S 300)

Galerina autumnalis   Deadly Galerina
Small brown caps fading to yellowish with a veil between cap edge and stalk leaving an evanescent ring on the stalks of mature specimens. Found singly or clustered on rotting wood, usually in late summer. Deadly poisonous.
(A 401; G 185; L 620; M 296; S 300)

D

Galerina sp.
Not identified beyond genus. A model LBM—difficult to identify to species and easily mistaken at first glance for possible membership in other troublesome genera. Small, brown, conical, translucent-striated caps, fading to yellowish as they dry. Common, scattered and in groups in deep moss under jack pine into late fall. Edibility unknown; could be poisonous.

E

Some mushrooms contain hallucinogens.
- In Lewis Carroll's *Adventures in Wonderland,* Alice, on advice from a caterpillar, nibbles at a mushroom and shrinks "to nine inches high."
- Some cultures considered hallucinogenic mushrooms to be sacred. The trance-like state induced by these mushrooms was believed to help priests communicate with the gods to foretell the future and obtain advice.

A

B

C

D

E

Gilled Fungi

Genus *Hebeloma*

Hebeloma crustuliniforme   Poison Pie
Caps mostly crust brown with lighter margins and viscid (slimy or sticky) when moist; mature gills brownish with serrated edges; top of stalk with surface granules; crushed flesh with radish-like odour. Singles and grouped; late summer; on ground under jack pine; mycorrhizal. Poisonous. Red berries are bunchberry (*Cornus canadensis*).
(A 464; L 624; M 300; S 302)

A

Hebeloma sinapizans   Scaly-Stalked Hebeloma
Faint pink in cap; thick, scaly stalk; radish-like odour. Spectacular blooms (many large rings of robust caps) under poplar and spruce following August rainy periods in some years; mycorrhizal. Poisonous.
(A 465; G 191; M 300; S 302)

B

Genus *Inocybe*

A group with many small, dull-coloured members. Typically the cap is knobbed or pointed and covered with a rough cuticle; spore print is brown. Several hundred species of *Inocybe* are catalogued for North America; most require microscopic examination for accurate identification. Members are terrestrial and mycorrhizal. Many are poisonous.
(A 455; G 183; M 301; S 303)

Genus *Rozites*

Inocybe sororia   Corn Silk Inocybe
An Inocybe easy to identify: straw-coloured, fibrillose cap with a prominent knob; the flesh when crushed often smells like newly husked green corn. Summer; on ground in mixed forest. Poisonous.
(A 457; L 632; S 303)

C

Rozites caperata   Gypsy Mushroom
The only member of the genus that is found in the boreal forest. Prominent ring on stalk; cap wrinkled and often showing a light hoary coating. Occasional large fruitings in thick moss under black spruce but also other habitats; midsummer to fall; mycorrhizal. Edible.
(A 412; G 187; L 635; M 302; S 311)

D

Family Entolomataceae

If the specimen has pink spores and gills attached to the stalk it is likely in this family; if it has pink spores and the gills are free from the stalk it is probably in genus *Pluteus*, family Plutaceae. Large members of the Entolomataceae are mostly in the genus *Entoloma*; small members mostly in *Nolanea*. A difficult family to work with based on field characters alone. Microscopic differences are important in sorting out species.
(A 238; L 640; S 288)

A

B

Mycophiles and Mycophobes

Why is it that some North Americans have a passion for wild mushrooms while others show an aversion to them? Much of this can be traced back to countries of origin. Mushroom picking has been called a national sport in some Asian and continental European countries. People from the United Kingdom, on the other hand, are generally seen as mycophobic. The name "toadstool," a less-than-complimentary word for mushroom, is usually identified with Great Britain.

C

D

Technical Vocabulary

Like all sciences, mushroom identification has its own terminology. Technically, the cap is the pileus, the gills (in gilled fungi) are the lamellae, the stalk is the stipe, the ring is the annulus. The membranous sack or scaly bulb at the base of the stalk of certain mushrooms, notably Amanitas, is the volva. A number of other terms that are in common use to describe finer points of mushroom identification are defined in the glossary, p. 97.

Genus *Entoloma*

Entoloma sp.
Not identified beyond genus. Look for pinkish, attached gills. Specimen on left covered with pinkish spores was underlying another cap. Found on ground in moss under jack pine and white spruce; late summer. Avoid eating because species is uncertain and there are some poisonous look-alikes.
(A 242; G 169; L 640; M 310; S 288)

A

Genus *Nolanea*

Nolanea mammosa   Bell-Shaped Nolanea
Small, nippled, striate cap; salmon-coloured gills; stately stalk. In feather moss under spruce and jack pine; summer and fall; saprophytic. Said to be poisonous.
(A 248; G 172; S 291)

B

Family Gomphidiaceae

An attractive and well-defined family with two easily recognizable genera; identification more difficult at species level. Look for distinctive shapes, blackish spores (sometimes traces on stalks) and decurrent gills (gills that are attached to and descend the stalk). Appear mainly after midsummer. Mycorrhizal with jack pine and spruce.
(A 481; G 219; L 649; M 314; S 203)

Genus *Chroogomphus*

Chroogomphus sp.   Pine Spikes
Not identified beyond genus. Spike-like body; flesh in cap pale orange, not white or greyish; base of stalk brownish, not bright yellow. At times common in needle beds under jack pine. Edible.
(A 484; L 649; M 314; S 204)

C

Genus *Gomphidius*

Gomphidius sp.   Slimy Pegs
Not identified beyond genus. Peg-like body; flesh in cap white to greyish, not pale orange; upper portion of stalk whitish, lower portion bright yellow. This genus is more common under spruce. Edible.
(A 481; G 219; L 649; M 316; S 204)

D

Family Hygrophoraceae   The Waxy Caps or Waxgills

A common and intriguing family of white-spored mushrooms in the northern forest. The soft, waxy texture of the gills (rub them between your fingers) is a diagnostic, if at times subtle, feature. The gills also are usually thick in appearance, well-spaced and attached to the stalk. Distinctive waxy caps in three genera—*Camarophyllus*, *Hygrocybe,* and *Hygrophorus*—are identified. Most members of the family bloom later in the season.
(A 103; G 131; L 654; M 196; S 231)

A

B

Tree Rotting Fungi

These are common members of forest communities. Their presence is revealed by fruiting bodies called conks and mushrooms. Roots, butts and trunks of living and dead trees are attacked and weakened, causing toppling and breaking. In most instances the actions of these fungi are considered normal features of a healthy forest. In plantations, however, some species cause considerable damage. (Source: *Forest Tree Diseases of the Prairie Provinces*. 1987. Y. Hiratsuka. Canadian Forestry Service.)

C

D

LBMs

Every major group of wild organisms has its confusing members, which are often grouped by the non-specialist under collective headings such as sparrows, canaries, mice and minnows. In the case of mushrooms, we have the LBMs or Little Brown Mushrooms. These are the many small species encountered on walks in the forest that stump even the experts. Some people find fault with the expression Little Brown Mushrooms because not all species difficult to identify are little and brown; many are big and white or some other combination of size and colour.

Genus *Camarophyllus*

Camarophyllus pratensis Meadow Waxgill
Orange in colour with widely spaced, arched
gills. Found in August in a grassy meadow
surrounded by jack pine; singles and in groups;
saprophytic. Edible.
(A 110; G 142; L 664; M 197; S 238)

A

Genus *Hygrocybe*

Hygrocybe conica Witch's Hat
Conical shape; colour variable in shades of
orange and yellow; cap and stalk turn black
when handled. Saprophytic on ground in a
variety of forest habitats; summer. Reported as
probably edible but not recommended because
of possible ill effects.
(A 116; G 139; L 658; M 198; S 237)

B

Genus *Hygrophorus*

Hygrophorus chrysodon Golden-Flaked Waxy
Cap
Cap and stalk whitish covered with golden
granules, especially around margin of cap and
apex of stalk. Late summer; in deep moss under
mixed jack pine and white spruce. Edible.
(A 119; G 138; L 657; M 204; S 233)

C

Hygrophorus discoideus Clay Waxy Cap
Questionable identity at level of species; can be
confused with look-alikes. Bull's-eye-like cap;
viscid cap and stalk. Common in groups in moss
and humus under white spruce; late summer and
fall. Edibility unknown.
(A 125; M 204)

D

Hygrophorus eburneus Ivory Waxy Cap
Pure white; exceptionally slimy—both cap and
stalk—when moist, shiny when dry. Late
summer; grouped on ground in mixed forest;
mycorrhizal. Edible. This white, all-viscid
species has attached, waxy gills. *H. piceae,* a
similar species, has a non-slimy stalk; *Limacella
illinita* has free, non-waxy gills.
(A 119; G 139; L 659; M 205; S 231)

E

Hygrophorus erubescens Reddening Waxgill
Purple-red cap often showing some yellow; no
cortina as on its common close relative,
H. purpurascens. Late summer under spruce;
mycorrhizal. Edibility unknown; not
recommended.
(A 124; L 667; M 206; S 234)

F

Hygrophorus olivaceoalbus Sheathed Waxy Cap
Slimy, grey-brown, streaked cap. The patterned
stalk below a collar-like ring makes this an
easily remembered waxy cap. Midsummer to
fall in moss under white spruce; mycorrhizal.
Reported as edible but not recommended.
(A 127; G 141; L 664; M 208; S 232)

G

Hygrophorus piceae Spruce Waxy Cap
Snow white; slimy cap, shiny when dry; non-
slimy stalk. Late summer in moss under spruce;
mycorrhizal. Edibility unknown.
(A 120; S 231)

H

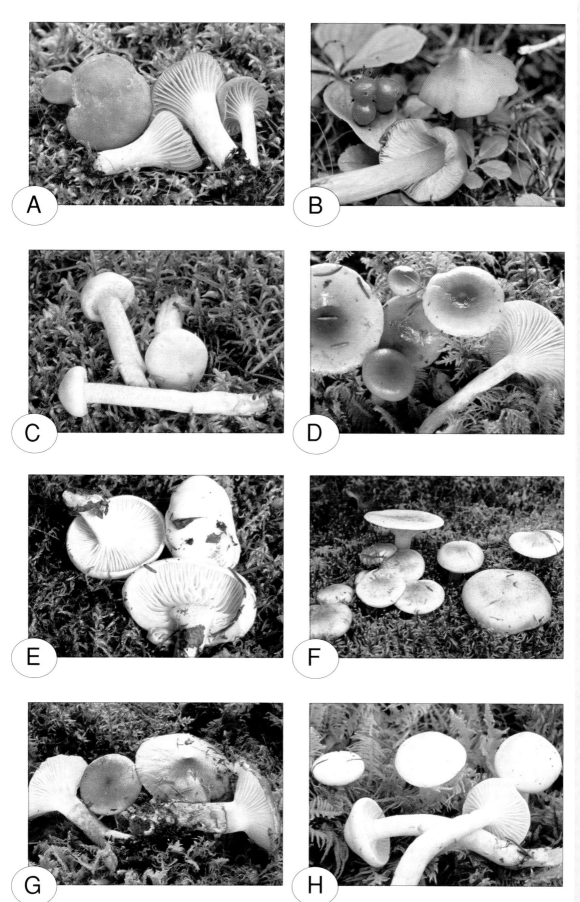

Hygrophorus purpurascens   Purple-Red Waxy Cap

Purple tones on whitish background; no yellow as on *H. erubescens*; with a faint Cortinarius-like cortina. Late summer under jack pine; mycorrhizal. Reported as edible but not recommended.
(A 124; G 144; L 667; M 206; S 234)

A

Hygrophorus speciosus   Larch Waxy Cap

A beautiful, bright orange-red to orange waxy cap; viscid cap and stalk. Solitary and grouped in moss under tamarack; uncommon. Late summer and fall; mycorrhizal. Edible.
(A 126; G 144; L 667; M 210)

B

Hygrophorus sp.
Not identified beyond genus since there are several look-alikes. I found this waxy cap to be exceptional due to its snow-white colour, its Russula-like appearance and its scattered occurrence in late summer and fall in reindeer moss (lichen) under open jack pine; mycorrhizal. Species uncertain; edibility unknown.

C

Hygrophorus sp.
Species of grey waxy caps are difficult to accurately sort out. This is an attractive mushroom with viscid, grey cap; white, decurrent (descending) gills; white stalk with faint grey speckles; no ring on stalk. Late summer and fall in feather moss under conifers; mycorrhizal. Edibility unknown.

D

Family Lepiotaceae
Lepiota is the sole genus placed here.
(A 293; M 239; S 222)

Genus *Lepiota*   Parasol Mushrooms
Some of the most beautiful mushrooms in the northern forest are found in this genus, but many are not easily identified at the species level. Gills are free from the stalk; spore prints are white. Terrestrial and saprophytic.
(A 293; G 94; M 239; S 222)

Lepiota clypeolaria   Shaggy-Stalked Parasol
A forest delight. Fragile; soft, cottony scales around edge of cap and below ring on stalk; brown disc at centre of cap. Summertime in various forest habitats. Poisonous.
(A 309; G 97; L 516; M 242; S 223)

E

Lepiota naucina   Smooth Parasol
White, smooth, helmet-shaped cap; distinct, persistent ring on stalk; no Amanita-like sack at base of stalk. Midsummer in grassy areas at edge of poplar and along grassy trails under poplar. Reported to be edible but not recommended because of possible confusion with deadly poisonous species.
(A 299; G 98; L 519; M 243; S 226)

F

A

B

C

D

Mushrooms in Arts and Crafts

Artists and photographers try to capture the beauty and variety of mushrooms in their work. Calendars, postcards and postage stamps from around the world often picture wild mushrooms. Craft shows almost always display drawings on woody polypores (commonly called conks) and feature dried mushrooms in floral arrangements. Mushrooms are popular subjects for wood carvings and ceramics. As the common names of some mushrooms indicate (e.g., Eastern Red-Dye, *Cortinarius semisanguineus, 10D*), they are the source of some beautiful dyes. More recently mushrooms have been used in paper making.

E

F

Lepiota rachodes   Shaggy Parasol
A large, distinctive Lepiota; brown scales on cap;
prominent ring on stalk; white flesh that quickly
bruises first orange then reddish. After
midsummer on disturbed ground in mixed stands
of white spruce and poplar. Edible with caution
because of possible ill effects. Before eating
make sure spore print is white, not green.
(A 297: G 97; L 521; M 246; S 224)

A

Lepiota sp.
Species uncertain. Scales are deep brown to
blackish; distinct ring is slender with blackish
edge. Summertime in feather moss under
black spruce. Edibility unknown; some
Lepiotas are deadly poisonous.

B

Lepiota sp.
Species uncertain. Scales are cinnamon
coloured and arranged in concentric bands;
stalk is cottony. Summertime in feather moss
under black spruce. Edibility unknown; may be
deadly poisonous.

C

On left, *Lilium philadelphicum* (wood lily);
on right, prime specimen of *Amanita fulva*
(Tawny Grisette), 4A. Western red lily, a
close relative to wood lily, is a Saskatchewan
emblem. Will there be a provincial mushroom
emblem some day?

Family Paxillaceae

Species are shown from two genera: *Hygrophoropsis* and *Paxillus*;
the former with white spore print, the latter with brown. This family
has an unstable history. One member, *Hygrophoropsis aurantiaca*
(False Chanterelle), with a white spore print, has been placed at
times in other families (Cantharellaceae and Tricholomataceae)
(A 476; L 668; M 312; S 205)

Genus *Hygrophoropsis*

Hygrophoropsis aurantiaca   False Chanterelle
Dark orange to orange-brown cap and bright
orange, forked gills distinguish this species.
Saprophytic on rotting coniferous stumps and
woody debris; summer. Reported as probably
edible but to be avoided because of possible ill
effects and similarity in appearance to poisonous
species.
(A 479; G 117; L 669; M 154; S 207)

D

Genus *Paxillus*

Paxillus vernalis   Spring Paxillus
A compact species; mottled, yellow-brown cap
with pronounced inrolled edge; gills forked near
the stalk; gills slowly stain a dark brown when
rubbed. Saprophytic on ground in early summer;
various forest habitats. Can be confused with its
look-alike, *P. involutus*. Edibility uncertain; not
recommended because of poisonous look-alike.
(A 478; L 671; S 206)

E

A

B

C

Gilled Fungi

A Provincial Mushroom Emblem

Some day Saskatchewan may select a mushroom as one of its official emblems to join with white birch, prairie sharp-tailed grouse and western red lily. The practice of naming an official mushroom was started by the State of Minnesota, which selected the Morel (*Morchella esculenta*), 78C2, as one of its symbols in 1984. A likely candidate for Saskatchewan is the Aspen Rough Stem or Red Cap (*Leccinum insigne*), 60A and p.93, a common species cherished by many pioneer homemakers for its edibility.

D

E

Family Plutaceae
All species presented are from the genus *Pluteus*.
(A 253; L 673; M 247; S 285)

Genus *Pluteus*
A very distinctive genus: free (not attached to the stalk), pinkish gills (from pink-coloured spores); no ring on the stalk; almost always on wood. (Family Entolomataceae has pink spores, gills attached to the stalk and is rarely on wood.) Largest number of specimens were found on dead, decomposing white birch and rotting poplar. Field characters alone are not always sufficient to accurately identify the many species in the genus. Microscopic features play an important role in describing individual members of *Pluteus*.
(A 254; G 165; L 673; M 248; S 285)

Pluteus admirabilis   Yellow Pluteus
Yellow cap and stalk. On rotting poplar log; summer. Reported to be edible but not recommended because of its questionable identity at level of species; can be confused with look-alikes.
(A 257; G 165; L 673; M 248)

A

Pluteus cervinus   The Deer Mushroom
Cap colour varies from dingy white to brown. This is the most common *Pluteus* in my experience. An early season mushroom and into summer; on rotting birch and poplar. Edible but double-check identification, making sure of genus.
(A 255; G 166; L 675; M 248; S 286)

B

Pluteus lutescens   Yellow-Stalked Deer Mushroom
Cap olive brown with ridges at the centre; striking lemon-yellow stalk. On rotting poplar; summer. Edibility unknown.
(A 257; M 251; S 286)

C

Pluteus patricius   Patrician Deer Mushroom
Grooved cap with brown streaks on a light background. On decomposing hardwoods; summer. Reported to be edible but double-check identification, making sure of genus.
(S 285)

D

Pluteus semibulbosus   Bulbous-Stalked Pluteus
Bell-shaped cap, off-white with cottony, silvery surface; stalk with a bulbous base. On rotting poplar log; summer. Species uncertain; edibility unknown.
(S 286)

E

Pluteus seticeps (Atk.) Singer*   Netted Pluteus
Brownish-black cap with netted surface; grey gills and stalk. Solitary and grouped on moist, rich humus under black spruce; late summer. Edibility unknown. (Identification by Dr. Scott Redhead.)
(A 258; L 677; M 250)

(* refer to box, top of page 25)

F

Credit Where Credit Is Due

Scientific names are recognized worldwide. A name is given to a species by the person who first describes the species in scientific literature. He or she is known as the author and his or her name is shown after the scientific name. Dr. Scott Redhead, at the National Mycological Herbarium, Ottawa, identified specimen 24F in this book as *Pluteus seticeps* (Atk.) Singer. Atkinson originally described this species. Singer later classified it differently. By rights, whenever scientific names are used they should include the name(s) of the scientist(s) who described and classified the species. However, many books today, including this one, that are designed for popular use adopt a shortened style that excludes the names of the authorities.

A

B

C

D

E

F

Gilled Fungi

Pluteus tomentosulus Small White Deer
(P. cervinus on right) Mushroom
White, woolly cap. On rotting birch and poplar;
summer. Edibility unknown.
(G 167; M 249; S 285)

A

Pluteus sp.
Not identified beyond genus because species
uncertain. Sturdy and impressive. Free gills;
pink spores. On rotting birch log; summer.
Edibility unknown.

B

Family Russulaceae   The Brittle Caps

A beginning mushroomer soon comes into contact with members of this family,
which appear in phenomenal numbers in some forest habitats following
midsummer rains. The brittle texture of the caps and stalks is a useful family
indicator. Bend the stalk of a prime specimen and it usually snaps like a piece of
chalk. Members are mycorrhizal with other forest growth. There are two genera:
Lactarius and *Russula*.
(A 63; G 37; L 679; S 207)

Family Russulaceae The Brittle Caps
An illustration of the brittle, chalk-like stalk that
is characteristic of the family. The mushroom is
Lactarius indigo, Indigo Milkcap, 28D.

C

Family Russulaceae
Russula means red; red members of the
genus *Russula* are sometimes common to
abundant in the northern forest. They never
fail to catch one's attention. Determining
the correct species, however, challenges
even the expert.

D

Genus *Lactarius*   The Milkcaps

This genus is known for the milk or latex that members exude when bruised or broken. Identification
at the species level can be troublesome but there are some highly distinctive members. The colour of
the latex, *when and after* it is exposed to air, is useful in sorting out species in this genus. Expose the
latex by bruising the gills or breaking the stalk at the gills. Watch for colour changes. (Note: some
species or specimens may show only very small amounts of latex).
(A 64; G 37; L 679; M 326; S 214)

A

B

New Mushroom Finds for Saskatchewan

In a 1989 article titled "A Biogeographical Overview of the Canadian Mushroom Flora" (Volume 67 of the *Canadian Journal of Botany*), Dr. S. A. Redhead mapped the known North American distribution of 74 mushroom species. There were no Saskatchewan records at the time for the following species.

Cantharellula umbonata, 34B   *Cystoderma cinnabarinum*, 40B

Tricholoma magnivelare, 50F   *Marasmius epiphyllus*, 44B

Rhodotus palmatus, 48H   *Marasmius pallidocephalus*, 44D

Lactarius indigo, 28D

C

D

Factors That May Affect the Flavour of Wild Mushrooms

- Some locations produce more flavour in mushrooms than do others. The Delicious Milkcap (*Lactarius deliciosus*), for example, is considered mediocre, at best, in some parts of the world but excellent in others.
- Preparation is frequently the key to good flavour. Japanese chefs don't throw expensive matsutakes into stew; special recipes are used to draw out the unique flavour of this prized mushroom. Even unpopular edibles, such as some species of *Suillus*, in the hands of experienced cooks can become delectable dishes.
- Mushrooms that grow on chemically treated substrates, such as urban lawns or roadside ditches, may be unpleasant to taste or even harmful.

A

Lactarius aspideoides   Bright Yellow Milkcap
Bright yellow, slimy cap; light yellow gills turn
purple when bruised. I came across this species
only twice, both times in colonies in leaf litter
and humus under willow; midsummer into fall.
Considered to be poisonous.
(A 76; S 220)

B

Lactarius controversus   Poplar Milkcap
A low, squat, whitish species; sticky when moist
and often dirty with ground debris; pinkish,
decurrent gills; latex white, unchanging when
exposed to air. Under poplar; late summer.
Inedible.
(A 70; G 42; L 681; S 215)

C

Lactarius deliciosus   Delicious Milkcap
A well-known milkcap. Cap orange, often zoned
with concentric rings. Carrot-orange latex that
discolours green. Abundant some years in a
variety of habitats; summer and fall. Edible.
(A 68; G 43; L 683; M 330; S 218)

D

Lactarius indigo   Indigo Milkcap
One of the most outstanding and memorable
mushrooms of the northern forest. The overall
blue colour, sometimes with greenish stains, and
the indigo-blue latex are especially striking.
Widely scattered under jack pine, frequently in
reindeer moss (lichen); moist summers. Edible.
(A 69; G 53; L 686; M 331)

E

Lactarius resimus   Yellow-Staining Bearded
Milkcap
Margin of whitish, sticky cap bearded with hairs;
white latex turns yellow when exposed to air.
Note the yellow staining on the bruised gills.
Late summer under spruce. Not edible.
(A 74; G 55; S 218)

F

Lactarius rufus   Red Hot Milkcap
Dull reddish-brown cap; stalk more lightly
coloured; latex white, unchanging. In groups
under jack pine and spruce often associated with
red squirrel middens; summer and early fall. Not
recommended for the table, may be poisonous.
(A 79; G 55; L 691; M 334; S 220)

G

Lactarius scrobiculatus   Pitted Milkcap
Cap pale yellow; stalk spotted; white latex turns
yellow on exposure. Late summer under conifers.
Not edible.
(A 73; G 56; L 692; M 335; S 217)

H

Lactarius torminosus   Bearded Milkcap
Very attractive woolly, peach-coloured cap; gills
with a pinkish tinge, often forked next to stalk;
latex white, unchanging. Mainly under live birch
(not found in dead stands, suggesting it dies
with its mycorrhizal host). Also found under
poplar; late summer. Considered to be
poisonous.
(A 73; G 57; L 694; M 337; S 215)

Lactarius uvidus   Purple-Staining Milkcap
Cap brown with shades of purple-grey; white latex; bruised gills slowly staining purple. Most sightings in midsummer under jack pine. Considered to be poisonous. Can be confused with other Milkcaps.
(A 75; G 58; L 695; M 339; S 217)

A

Lactarius sp.
Not identified beyond genus; look-alikes are a problem. Cap brown; stalk cream coloured with shallow irregular pitting, hollow; latex white, unchanging. A common midsummer Milkcap in feather moss under jack pine. Edibility unknown.

B

Genus *Russula*   The Russulas

If the stalk snaps like a piece of chalk when broken, and there is no latex, it is probably a Russula. After settling that in the affirmative, one's patience with this group's members will probably be tested many times. They appear in a wide spectrum of overlapping and inconsistent colours, singly and in groups, in most habitats, and oftentimes are large and in the forefront of fungi in the forest. The problem is that many species defy identification. Suggestions for dealing with the Russulas include: know and appreciate them as a group; identify the occasional member; leave the rest for the specialists.
(A 83; G 60; L 679; M 317; S 208)

Russula brevipes   Short-Stalked Russula
Not one of the colourful Russulas. It is dull white, sturdy, short-stalked and often soiled. As the caps push up from the depths they carry moss and ground debris with them. Common under jack pine, also in other habitats; summer. Considered edible but not recommended because of possible ill effects and confusion with other species.
(A 87; L 698; M 318; S 214)

C

Russula chamaeleontina   Small Yellow Russula
Small, deep yellow caps; white stalks. Scattered under poplar; midsummer. Edible. There is some uncertainty regarding the correct scientific name or names for small yellow Russulas.
(A 101; G 64; S 210)

D

Russula densifolia   Reddening Russula
Cap whitish, aging to brownish black; gills close, off-white aging to smoky brown; flesh white, bruising reddish slowly. Groups in needle litter and moss under jack pine; summer and fall. Not recommended for the table.
(A 90; G 65; L 701; M 319; S 214)

E

Russula nigricans   Blackening Russula
Cap dirty brown; gills thick, well spaced, brittle, with veins and forks; stalk firm, white, staining red when scraped and then black. Groups in duff under jack pine; late summer and fall. Inedible.
(A 90; G 65; L 701; M 319; S 214)

F

A

B

Insects and Mushrooms

The bane of mushroom hunters in the forest is insects. They bite and bug your person while their larvae are munching on the mushrooms you may be planning to have for supper. The solution to the latter is to pick before the larvae arrive or, as some mushroomers suggest, rid the caps of larvae before cooking. A few larval tunnels in the mushrooms are not noticeable after cooking and do not affect the flavour.

C

D

E

F

Gilled Fungi

Russula xerampelina   Shrimp Russula
Colour variable around reds, purples and
browns; gills yellowish; stalk usually with
pinkish tinge; odour of shrimp or fish when
mature. Scattered under jack pine; late summer.
Edible but double-check identification because
confusion can arise with other species.
(A 102; G 76; L 707; M 325; S 209)

A

Russula spp.
Three colourful Russulas from jack pine
forest. Each occurs in pure colonies;
midsummer. Species uncertain; edibilities
unknown.

B

Family Strophariaceae

Two genera are represented: *Pholiota* and *Stropharia*. This family also contains
the much-publicized hallucinogenic mushrooms in the genus *Psilocybe*.

Genus *Pholiota*

A large, brown-spored genus including some beautiful, clumped, yellow species,
but many require microscopic examination for identification. A major decomposer
of both deciduous and coniferous wood; some species are parasitic on living trees.
(A 384; G 184; M 270; S 318)

Pholiota destruens   Destructive Pholiota
Whitish, scaly cap and stalk; stalk thick and
firm; older gills brown from spores. A robust
destroyer of poplar logs; late summer. Edible
but not recommended.
(A 395; L 714; S 320)

C

Pholiota squarrosa   Scaly Pholiota
Yellow-brown cap and stalk; ring on stalk. One
of scaliest mushrooms in the forest. Usual find
is a striking cluster at the base of a live poplar;
midsummer. A strong odour of garlic often
associated with this species. Poisonous.
(A 389; G 189; L 716; M 272; S 321)

D

Genus *Stropharia*

Stropharia aeruginosa   Blue-Green Stropharia
A unique blue-green mushroom, sometimes
with dark purplish spores adhering to stalk. In
moss under spruce in late summer; saprophytic.
Toxicity uncertain; not recommended because
of possible ill effects.
(A 380; G 204; L 725; M 262; S 317)

E

Stropharia semiglobata   Dung Roundhead
Yellow rounded cap; stalk long and fragile,
often with ring blackened by spores. (Note the
flimsy blackened ring on right specimen).
Appears shortly after summer rains. Usually
associated with domestic animal manure.
Picture shows specimens on moose droppings
in a black spruce forest. Edible but not
recommended.
(A 376; G 205; L 730; M 266; S 316)

F

A

B

Rocket Fuel

The unusual chemistry of some mushrooms is clearly illustrated by the False Morel (*Gyromitra esculenta*), 80D. This species is made deadly poisonous for humans by its content of gyromitrin, a constituent of rocket fuel. Although not worth the risk, some people cook and eat this mushroom. Parboiling, it is said, volatilizes and drives off the chemical. The released fumes, however, have been known to poison the cook.

C

D

E

F

Gilled Fungi

Family Tricholomataceae

A diversified family with many genera and species; white to pale-coloured spores. There is no outstanding feature that distinguishes members of this family such as the waxiness of the Hygrophoraceae and the brittleness of the Russulaceae. It compares in complexity with the brown-spored Cortinariaceae.
(A 129; L 731; M 133; S 239)

Genus *Armillaria*

Armillaria mellea   Honey Mushroom
A complex species with several variants. Cap honey-coloured, scaly or smooth; stalk with a cottony ring. One of the most interesting mushrooms in the northern forest; it is not only attractive but also intriguing, appearing at odd times, in odd manners and in odd places. Solitary specimens occur but the memorable growths are large clumps (dusted with white spores) on stumps and other dead wood and at the base of live poplar trees. Both saprophytic and parasitic; late summer and fall; it has its good years (e.g., 1995) and its poor years (e.g., 1993). A "good" year for this and many other species is often cause for amazement because until it is experienced one has no idea just how abundant and widespread a particular fungus actually is. The honey mushroom is intriguing for yet another reason: an observer, in the dark of night, may see a luminous glow from wood that contains the mycelium of this species. Edible and popular but caution is advised because identification at times can be tricky and because of possible ill effects.
(A 196; G 101; L 736; M 136; S 256)

A1

A2

Genus *Cantharellula*

Cantharellula umbonata   Grayling
An unassuming but attractive species with greyish cap and strongly forked gills that stain reddish in age. In moss under jack pine and other conifers; sometimes forming rings. Late summer and fall; saprophytic. Considered to be edible but double-check identity.
(A 165; G 36; L 741; S 269)

Cypripedium passerinum (Franklin's lady's slipper). A beautiful summer flower of moist coniferous forests, usually coinciding with first major flush of forest mushrooms.

B

Genus *Clitocybe*   The Clitocybes

A large, common, saprophytic genus with many indistinct species. Clitocybe means "sloping head." Many members of this genus do have funnel-shaped caps and gills running down the stalk but so do some members of other genera. It is a useful starting point, however. Thick, white mycelium attached to the stalk and permeating the substrate is also a useful if not steadfast property of this genus.
(A 148; G 107; M 138; S 245)

Mushroom Succession

Some species of mushrooms appear after others as a log or stump slowly decomposes. Exact sequences from pioneer to terminal species are difficult to establish but some species prefer sound wood, others are found on humus, while still others occur on in-between stages of woody decomposition. Succession of mushroom species is also seen as a forest matures from newly burned to old growth.

A1

A2

B

Gilled Fungi

Carnivorous Fungi

A trick employed by some plants, notably pitcher plants and Venus' flytraps, is to obtain nitrogen by capturing and digesting mosquitoes, flies and other small insects. Recently, researchers at the University of Guelph have discovered that mycelial filaments of some fungi employ the same technique by attacking and consuming microscopic organisms found in great abundance in rotting wood and soil. Predation, therefore, must be recognized as another survival mechanism for some saprophytic fungi.

Clitocybe albirhiza   Snowmelt Clitocybe
Pale buff, thin cap; gills descending stalk in age.
Questionable identity at level of species; there
are similar appearing Clitocybes. When it is
lifted from substrate, note the dense mass of
white mycelial threads, intertwined with spruce
needles, at the base of the stalk. Solitary and in
groups; in moss and rich humus under black
spruce; late spring. Edibility unknown.
(A 161; M 138)

A

Clitocybe gibba   Funnel Mushroom
Tan, funnel-shaped cap with gills running down
the stalk. Its shape suggests the genus; in fact,
the original description of the genus *Clitocybe*
was based on this species. Solitary and in groups
in several forest habitats; midsummer. Edible
but not recommended because of possible
confusion with species of unknown edibility.
(A 157; G 121; L 747; M 141; S 250)

B

Clitocybe maxima   Large Funnel Cap
Resembles *Clitocybe gibba*, but more robust with
larger cap and thicker stalk. Often in rings or
rows; mixed-forest habitats; summer. Edible but
not recommended because of possible confusion
with species of unknown edibility.
(A 157; G 123; L 748; M 141; S 250)

C

Clitocybe nebularis   Cloudy Clitocybe
Greyish-brown cap; gills slightly descending
stalk; thick, white mycelium under base of stalk.
Pale yellow spore print. Disagreeable odour. In
rows, rings and groups on humus under mature
mixed spruce and poplar; occasionally abundant;
summer. Considered poisonous.
(A 159; G 118; L 749; M 142; S249)

D

Clitocybe odora   Blue-Green Anise Mushroom
Light green cast to young specimens; odour
strongly fragrant. Both scattered individuals and
in rings, with noticeable mycelium; under white
spruce and poplar; late summer. Distinctive
features such as this species' colour and odour
are unusual for a Clitocybe. Edible.
(A 161; G 122; L 750; M 144; S 247)

E

This mushroom, a member of the genus
Leucopaxillus (p. 42), was unearthed to reveal
the thick, white mycelial mat at the base of
the stalk. The mycelium is growing in a rich
layer of forest humus. Some groups, such as
the Russulaceae, reveal little mycelium.

Genus *Collybia*

The name "Collybia" means "small coin" and this often comes to mind when members
of the genus are seen on the forest floor. This is another genus where distinctiveness,
with few exceptions, is not a strong trait. Six of the more easily identified species are
pictured. All are saprophytic.
(A 201; G 149; M 147; S 251)

A

B

C

D

E

A Strange One

The Inky Cap (*Coprinus atramentarius*), 6C, is described by Groves (1979) as a "...very desirable edible species," subject, as several authors point out, to one major reservation: do not consume this mushroom with, before or after, any alcoholic beverage. The combination of this species and alcohol in the body results in disagreeable reactions: reddening in the face, tingling in the extremities, fast heartbeat, and possibly headache and nausea. Recovery is usually within a few hours.

Collybia acervata Clustered Collybia
Occurs in tight bundles on rotting spruce; reddish-brown stalks; thick, white mycelium at base of cluster; late summer. As caps lose moisture their colour fades from reddish brown to tan. Inedible due to bitter taste and suspected ill effects.
(A 215; G 150; L 753; M 147; S 252)

A

Collybia butyracea Butter Collybia
Reddish-brown cap and stalk; cap greasy (buttery) when moist; stalk often fibrous, striated and twisted. Pinkish-buff spore print helps to confirm identity. Scattered to grouped under conifers; late summer. Edible but not recommended because of possible misidentification.
(A 216; G 151; L 755; M 147; S 252)

B

Collybia confluens Tufted Collybia
Cap reddish brown fading to tan; gills crowded; stalk reddish brown, felty. Caps shrivel when dry, open when moist. In clusters on litter under spruce; summer. Collybias are subject to misidentification. Edible with caution; double-check identity.
(A 213; G 151; L 754; M 148; S 252)

C

Collybia dryophila June Mushroom
Very common on forest floor in spring and early summer, sometimes forming rings and rows; underlain with a whitish mycelial mat. As caps dry and age, their colour changes from reddish brown to buff. Edible but not recommended because of occasional ill effects. An occasional group has members covered with lumps of the fungus *Christiansenia mycetophila* known as Collybia Jelly, 84C.
(A 215; G 151; L 755; M 149; S 252)

D

Collybia maculata Spotted Collybia
Whitish cap and stalk with reddish stains; often with a long stalk extending deep—root-like—into substrate. Solitary and grouped, sometimes in clusters of two or three; in moss under jack pine; late summer. Edible but not recommended.
(A 217; G 152; L 756; M 150; S 253)

E

Collybia tuberosa Tuberous Collybia
Off-white, dainty species grouped on blackened remains of old mushrooms; mainly in the fall. Edibility unknown.
(A 212; G 157; L 757; M 151)

F

Genus *Cystoderma*
Members of this genus have caps coated with fine, mealy granules; saprophytic.
(A 198; G 100; S 270)

Gilled Fungi

A

B

C

D

E

F

Random Thoughts

- Keep the fun in fungi. (David Arora)
- Life is too short to stuff a mushroom. (Author Unknown)
- Mushrooms are where and when you find them. (Anonymous)
- Any mushroom guide can only contain a limited number of species (Helene M.E. Schalkwijk-Barendsen)
- Why did God make so many mushrooms? (Six-year old Roddy Herzog)

Cystoderma amianthinum Common Cystoderma
Yellowish-brown, granular cap. A petite forest
"weed." Mostly late summer and fall in moss
under jack pine and spruce. A colony of white
forms was found on one occasion. Reported as
probably edible but not recommended because
of resemblance to poisonous species.
(A 200; G 100; L 510; M 152; S 271)

A

Cystoderma cinnabarinum Vermilion
Cystoderma
A beautiful species with rusty-orange, granular
cap and rusty-orange, scaly stalk. Common
some summers, rare others; scattered in moss
and on needle mat under black spruce. Reported
as edible but of poor quality.
(A 200; G 100; M 152; S 271)

B

Genus *Flammulina*

Flammulina velutipes Velvet Foot
Sticky (when moist), yellow-brown caps; older
specimens with rusty-brown, velvety stems. In
clusters on buried roots and rotting poplar logs;
summer. Edible.
(A 220; G 158; L 759; M 152; S 266)

C

Genus *Hemimycena*

Hemimycena gracilis Slender White Bog
Mushroom
Identification uncertain. Small, all-white
species. In groups on the dark forest floor
under black spruce. Saprophytic, each
mushroom often arising from a spruce needle;
summer. Edibility unknown.
(S 273)

D

Genus *Hypsizygus*

Hypsizygus tessulatus Elm Oyster
Identification uncertain. White, robust,
conspicuous fall mushroom emerging from
wounds on live poplar; stalks are curved; gills
are not decurrent, i.e., do not run down the
stalk. Not to be confused with *Pleurotus
ostreatus* (Oyster Mushroom), 48G, whose gills
descend the stalk. Edibility unknown.
(A 133; G 106; L 761)

E

Genus *Laccaria*

Laccaria laccata Orange Laccaria
Variable mushroom that shows up in different
habitats, from sandy soils under jack pine to
moss beds under spruce. Usually readily
recognized by its orange colour, well-spaced
gills (often dusted with white spores), and tough
stalks that may appear overbuilt for the small
caps. Some authors suggest we may be dealing
with several look-alike species. Edible but not
recommended because of possible confusion
with other species.
(A 172; G 145; L 762; M 156; S 279)

F1

Genus *Neolentinus*

Same species as F1.
The mushrooms in F1 are growing in
sphagnum moss under tamarack and black
spruce, while those in F2 are in feather moss
under jack pine. Habitats are so different one
might expect the two to be separate species.
The truth will be known some day.

F2

Neolentinus lepideus Train Wrecker
Tough, durable mushroom; off-white cap with
brownish scales; gills with serrated edges;
membranous ring on stalk. Decomposes both
deciduous and coniferous logs, including
railroad ties, hence its common name. Some
resemblance to dark-spored *Pholiota destruens*
(Destructive Pholiota), 32C, but the Train
Wrecker has white spores, serrated gills and is
found most frequently on coniferous wood.
Edible.
(A 142; G 161; L 766; M 159; S 283)

G

Genus *Lepista*

Three species are pictured. All are saprophytic; found on moss and humus. Yellowish to pinkish-buff spore prints help to confirm identities. Some authors place these species in genus *Clitocybe*.
(A 148; G 124; S 257)

Lepista inversa   Orange Funnel Cap
Attractive dull-orange cap and stalk; long descending gills, remindful of the genus *Clitocybe*. Grouped in moss under spruce; midsummer. Not recommended for the table.
(A 156; M 141; S 257)

A

Lepista irina   Woolly Lepista
Off-white, robust cap often with a characteristic low dome; whitish stalk. Spectacular fruitings some autumns in moist situations under mixtures of spruce, poplar and willow; arising from dense mycelial mats. Reported as edible but not recommended because of possible ill effects and confusion with poisonous species.
(A 155; G 126; L 750; M 141; S 257)

B

Lepista nuda   Blewit
Bluish, robust cap and stalk. Several forest habitats; sometimes in rings and arcs; thick, white mycelium in moss and duff. Mid- to late-summer. A well-known and popular edible. "Blewit" comes from "blue hat."
(A 153; G 127; L 749; M 143; S 258)

C

Genus *Leucopaxillus*

Leucopaxillus giganteus   Giant Leucopax
The mature, platter-size, white caps present a memorable sight especially when they occur in long rows. Underlain by dense mycelium in rich organic matter; under white spruce and poplar; mid- to late-summer; saprophytic. Edible but not highly recommended.
(A 159; G 123; L 748; S 260)

D1

Long rows or arcs of *Leucopaxillus giganteus* (Giant Leucopax) create summer spectacles in the forest. Are these isolated rows? If so, why did the fungi travel in lines? Or are they arcs— remnants of large rings that began in the centre a long time past?

D2

Leucopaxillus piceinus   Spruce Leucopax
Rounded, cream-coloured to tan, solid caps; copious mycelium in rich duff under mature white spruce. Occurs in rings, arcs and loose aggregations; midsummer; saprophytic. Edible but not highly recommended.
(G 122; S 259)

E

Sole or Joint Occupancy

Questions arise concerning the fungal occupants of a log or stump when a single species is seen crowding the surface. Can a stump or log be host to more than one species of mushroom? Perhaps some species of fungi can exclude others, but it is not unusual to see a woody substrate harbouring more than one kind of mushroom. Mushroomers revisiting special sites occasionally note a spring mushroom followed by a summer species on the same log or stump.

A

B

C

D1

D2

E

Gilled Fungi

Genus *Lyophyllum*

Lyophyllum decastes   Fried Chicken Mushroom
A complex species with several variants. Cap colour ranging from grey to brown. Occurs in large groups of massive clumps; midsummer; saprophytic. Most authors mention grassy areas, roadsides and waste places as habitats; my records are for a dry, hummocky bog under black spruce. Derivation of the common name is not explained. Edible with caution because of possible confusion with poisonous species.
(A 174; G 121; L 768; M 163; S 263)

A1

Same species as A1. A large gathering of this clumped species in the forest presents a mushroom spectacle that rivals any other. This species has white spores. Some poisonous Entolomas, with pink spores, also grow in clumps.

A2

Genus *Marasmius*

Many members of this genus, including the three that are pictured, shrivel up and virtually disappear during dry spells, only to revive in all their splendour with the next rain.
(A 201; G 158; M 165; S 253)

Marasmius epiphyllus   White Pinwheel
Small, white, wrinkled cap with well-spaced gills. Common and conspicuous on rotting poplar leaves following late summer and fall rains, often in association with fairy hair (*Macrotyphula juncea*), 68D. Not recommended for eating.
(A 206; S 254)

B

Marasmius oreades   Fairy Ring Mushroom
Tan cap; well-spaced gills; tough stalk; often forming rings in lawns. Although not a true forest mushroom, it is included here because it is so well known and is often seen where lawns are maintained in the northern forest. Appears in early summer. Edible with caution because of resemblance to poisonous species and because of possible contamination with lawn chemicals.
(A 208; G 159; L 772; M 166; S 255)

C

Marasmius pallidocephalus   Conifer Pinwheel
Cap reddish brown to off-white; stalk dark brown, hair-like. In groups in needle duff under conifers; stalks individually attached to conifer needles, twigs, cones; summer. Inconspicuous when shrivelled up during dry spells but eye-catching when caps expand following rains. Edibility unknown.
(A 208; M 165; S 253)

D1

A saprophytic fungus (*Marasmius pallidocephalus*, Conifer Pinwheel). Each stalk attached to one or more black spruce needles; mycelium seen as black filaments intertwined with needles.

D2

A1

A2

Reindeer Moss (*Cladonia* spp.)

A distinctive grey-green ground cover occurring in extensive beds on dry, sandy soils under open jack pine. Several species of mushrooms are found in these beds (see 20C, 50F, 54A, 80D). Reindeer moss is actually a lichen, an unusual, hardy organism consisting of a fungus and a photosynthetic alga. Woodland caribou ("reindeer") may have fed in these areas in the past. Walking in dry reindeer moss can damage it and should be avoided.

B

C

D1

D2

Gilled Fungi

Genus *Melanoleuca*

Mostly stately species with tall, straight, slender stalks, and close to crowded gills. Several require microscopic examination for positive identification. Members of the genus are reported to be saprophytic.
(A 169; G 130; M 169; S 260)

Melanoleuca alboflavida Yellowish Melanoleuca
Cap yellowish brown; gills white, thin and crowded; stalk rigid and straight. Pictured specimens are in a partial ring under mixed white spruce and poplar; late summer; not common. Melanoleucas are subject to misidentification. Edible but double-check identity.
(A 169; G 131; L 776; M 169; S 261)

A

Melanoleuca cognata Peach-Gilled Melanoleuca
Brown to pale-tan cap; peach-coloured, crowded gills; tall and slender stalk. Early season; terrestrial; under mixed forest—spruce, poplar, white birch. Reported to be edible but not recommended because it belongs to a confusing genus.
(A 170; S 262)

B

Melanoleuca melaleuca Dark Melanoleuca
Blackish cap contrasting with white gills; straight, slender stalk. Impressive autumn species. May be found in moss beds under spruce. Reported to be edible but not recommended because it is a member of a group that is difficult to sort out.
(A 169; G 131; L 777; M 169; S 261)

C

Birch trees and fungi. The fungi of birch are a study in themselves. Dead and live stands of birch possess a bewildering array of saprophytic, mycorrhizal and parasitic mushrooms. This picture shows four specimens of a *Pluteus* (p. 24) competing for space on the broken end of a well-rotted birch log.

Genus *Mycena* The Mycenas

The warblers of the mushroom world—diminutive, attractive, diverse and difficult to identify and remember. Young specimens mostly with conical to bell-shaped caps. A white-spored genus, not to be confused with several small, Mycena-like, dark-spored mushrooms. Saprophytes on logs, stumps, needles, leaves, duff; sometimes in beautiful masses. Mycenas as a group are best left to advanced mushroomers or specialists for identification. Four distinctive species are shown.
(A 224; G 147; M 170; S 272)

Much folklore is grounded in mushroom formations and shapes.

- Some species form eye-catching rings or circles. It is said these rings are peopled by fairies who, on warm summer nights, dance in the centres and rest on the surrounding stools.
- The resemblance of many small woodland mushrooms to human articles contributed to the notion that forests are peopled by elves and fairies. Common names of mushrooms include fairy fans, fairy cups, fairy clubs, fairy hair, fairy stools, elfin cups and elfin saddles.

A

B

C

Gilled Fungi

- Other names, such as "witch's butter" for some jelly mushrooms and "devil's snuff box" for puffballs, conjure up evil spirits.
- Erotic, phallic-shaped mushrooms are steeped in European myth and folklore. It is said they were used in fertility rites and as love potions and aphrodisiacs.

48

Mycena haematopus Bleeding Fairy Helmet
A beautiful reddish-brown species that exudes a blood-red juice when cut. Pictured specimens are bunched on the broken end of a rotting birch log; summer. Edible, but its small size discourages picking.
(A 231; L 781; M 173; S 275)

A

Mycena lilacifolia Lilac Mycena
An early season, eye-catching, yellow Mycena with lilac tints; slimy when moist; descending gills. Clustered on rotting conifer stumps and logs. Edibility unknown.
(A 236; L 740; M 174)

B

Mycena overholtzii Snowbank Fairy Helmet
Cap colour ranges from grey to bluish grey to brown. Distinctive because of its large size (for a Mycena), its appearance in early spring (as early as last days of April some years) when there are still remnants of snow drifts in the forest, and the dense, white hairs along the base of the stalk. Look for clusters on well-rotted spruce stumps and logs. Edibility unknown.
(A 234; L 783; M 175)

C

Mycena pura Pink Mycena
One of largest Mycenas; lilac to pinkish coloured caps, stalks and gills. Scattered (not clumped) on forest litter and feather moss; mainly under spruce; summer. Edibility uncertain; possibly poisonous.
(A 230; G 149; L 784; M 175; S 277)

D

Genus *Oudemansiella*

Oudemansiella longipes Deep Root
Greyish-brown velvety cap and stalk; white, well-spaced gills. This specimen deeply rooted into rotten poplar stump. Summer. Edible.
(A 220; G 157; L 789; M 179)

E

Genus *Phyllotopsis*

Phyllotopsis nidulans Smelly Oyster
A very distinctive saprophytic species. Shelving, pale-orange masses on rotting logs and stumps of birch, spruce and poplar. Sewer gas odour is diagnostic. Middle to late season; sometimes overwinters appearing fresh in spring. Reported as non-poisonous but repulsive odour does not recommend it.
(A 140; G 179; L 791; M 181; S 281)

F

Genus *Pleurotus*

Pleurotus ostreatus Oyster Mushroom
White, shelving clusters; fruiting from ground level on fallen poplar logs to high up on dead standing trees; mainly in spring and early summer; home to a prolific, small, brown-and-black beetle. Is this the most important decomposer of dead poplar in the northern forest? It is certainly one of the showiest. Common most years, abundant in some. Edible, see recipe section, pp.92-96.
(A 134; G 105; L 793; M 181; S 281)

G

Genus *Rhodotus*

Rhodotus palmatus Netted Rhodotus
Cap red to pink with network of raised surface veins. One of most beautiful and distinctive mushrooms of the northern forest. Occurs on rotting poplar logs in mature white spruce and poplar stands during summer; not common. Edibility unknown.
(A 130; G 106; L 795; M 183; S 280)

H

Gilled Fungi

Genus *Tricholoma*   The Triches

A prominent and impressive white-spored genus of fungi in the northern forest. It takes a while to grasp this large, well-represented, diverse group. A diagnostic feature to look for is a small, variable notch on the gills at point of attachment to the stalk. (For illustration, see 50C). This is not an unfailing trademark but it is often present and often indicates *Tricholoma*. Species are most common in late summer and fall; said to be mycorrhizal with various trees. Eleven members of the genus are illustrated; be on the lookout for others.
(A 176; G 124; M 185; S 240)

Tricholoma caligatum   Fragrant Tricholoma
Brownish fibers and scales on cap and on stalk below ring; odour sometimes spicy-fruity. Under jack pine; late summer. Reported as edible but not recommended because of possible confusion with other members of the genus.
(A 192; L 732; M 134)

A

Tricholoma cingulatum   Willow Tricholoma
Small, blue-grey Tricholoma; ring on the stalk. May be found under willow; late summer. Edibility unknown.
(A 177; S 244)

B

Tricholoma flavovirens   Man on Horseback
A striking yellow species with sticky cap, when moist, and white flesh. Notched gills are evident. Under a variety of trees but best records are from moss beds under jack pine in late fall. Yes, the common name is unusual; maybe they were hunted at one time by men on horseback; or did they remind someone of a cavalier or knight? Edible.
(A 179; G 125; L 800; M 186; S 242)

C

Tricholoma imbricatum   Shingled Tricholoma
Dry, brown cap that may show scales in age; no ring; stalk white with brown stains over lower portion. Singles and groups in moss and needle mat under jack pine; late summer and fall. Not recommended for the table because of possible confusion with poisonous Tricholomas.
(A 186; G 127; L 800; M 187)

D

Tricholoma inamoenum Ill-Scented Tricholoma
White to creamy, small caps; odour of moth balls. Common after midsummer in moss under spruce. Inedible; possibly poisonous.
(A 179; M 188; S 244)

E

Tricholoma magnivelare   Matsutake or Pine Mushroom
Robust, white mushroom; prominent band on stalk; distinctive spicy odor. It erupts from the depths of sandy soils in beds of reindeer moss (lichens) under older jack pine; moist summers. Edible. If the word "proud" may be applied to a mushroom, this species' appearance in the forest would qualify.
(A 191; L 733; M 135; S 241)

F

Peat Moss (*Sphagnum* spp.)

Thick beds of peat moss occur in boggy sites associated with tamarack and black spruce (see 40F1, 54B2). As is true of other habitats, sphagnum beds are favoured by some species of mushrooms. The Trumpet Chanterelle (*Cantharellus tubaeformis*), 54B, an alluring species, is often found on sphagnum hummocks.

A

B

C

D

E

F

Gilled Fungi

A

Tricholoma portentosum   Streaked Tricholoma
Grey, streaked, sticky cap; gills and stalk tinged greenish yellow. Scattered in moss under jack pine; late summer and fall; uncommon. Edible but not recommended because of possible confusion with poisonous Tricholomas.
(A 180; L 803; M 189)

B

Tricholoma saponaceum   Soapy Tricholoma
This can be a difficult species to recognize but usually there are greenish shades on the cap and pinkish flesh near base of stalk. Scattered or grouped under spruce, poplar and jack pine; summer and fall. Inedible.
(A 184; G 128; L 804; M 190; S 242)

C

Tricholoma vaccinum   Scaly Tricholoma
Reddish-brown scaly cap; wide fringe of tissue around edge of cap that hugs the stalk on young specimens. Common and abundant some summers in groups under jack pine and spruce. Inedible; may be poisonous.
(A 186; G 130; L 805; M 191; S 244)

D

Tricholoma virgatum   Fibril Tricholoma
Greyish cap with distinctive pointed knob. Remindful of an Inocybe but Inocybes have brown spores. A handsome mushroom with little resemblance to most other members of the genus. Scattered or grouped; often in moss beds under jack pine and spruce; late summer and fall. Edibility uncertain; may be poisonous.
(A 181; G 129; L 806; M 192)

Genus *Tricholomopsis*

E

Tricholoma zelleri   Zeller's Mushroom
Orange-brown, streaked cap; no scales; stalk orange-brown below conspicuous ring. Late summer under spruce and jack pine. Reported as edible but not recommended because of possible confusion with other Tricholomas.
(A 188; L 735; M 193; S 240)

F

Tricholomopsis rutilans   Plums and Custard
Reddish hairs on yellow caps and stalks and bright yellow gills bring to mind the common name. Prime specimens rank with the most striking mushrooms in the northern forest. Saprophytes on rotting spruce logs and stumps; summer and fall. Edible but not highly rated.
(A 145; G 128; L 808; M 194; S 266)

Genus *Xeromphalina*

G

Xeromphalina campanella   Orange Fuzzyfoot
Small, brownish-orange, non-slimy cap; gills descending stalk; stalk yellowish at apex, reddish brown below. A memorable sight when found in dense clusters on tops and sides of decaying, moss-covered white spruce and jack pine stumps and logs. Often makes early spring appearances. Reported as non-poisonous but lowly rated as an edible species.
(A 222; G 146; L 809; M 195; S 274)

H

Xeromphalina fraxinophila   Rufus Fuzzyfoot
Small, yellow-brown cap; yellowish, descending gills; dark brown stalk. Scattered and gregarious on forest litter; various habitats; fall. Edibility unknown.
(S 274)

Ridged Fungi
(Undersurfaces of caps have gill-like ridges or folds but not true gills)

Family Cantharellaceae   The Chanterelles

This is the only family placed in the Ridged Fungi. The distinction between "true gills" and "gill-like ridges or folds" may not be quickly evident but is revealed on careful examination. Two genera are featured: *Cantharellus* and *Gomphus*. The Golden Chanterelle (Cantharellus cibarius), 54A, is of economic importance to northern Saskatchewan and is one of the best known and most highly prized edible mushrooms in the world.
(A 658; L 387; M 81; S 358)

Genus *Cantharellus*

Cantharellus cibarius   Golden Chanterelle
Orange-yellow and firm overall; cap smooth often with inrolled wavy margin, bleaching in sunlight; not true gills but thick gill-like forked ridges descending sturdy stalk. In northern Saskatchewan, scattered and in groups in reindeer moss (lichen) under jack pine; mid-July to freeze-up under favourable conditions; mycorrhizal. A choice edible, but confirm identity; there are toxic look-alikes.
   (A 662; G 33; L 387; M 81; S 358)

A

Cantharellus tubaeformis Trumpet Chanterelle
Caps yellowish brown, funnel-shaped with hollow centres; undersurfaces with gill-like shallow ridges. To search for this species one has to abandon jack pine hills, pass through white spruce and poplar lowlands and go deep into black spruce and tamarack bogs. Found in groups on sphagnum hummocks; late summer and fall. Edible with caution because of possible ill effects.
   (A 665; G 35; L 392; M 84; S 359)

B1

Genus *Gomphus*

Same species as B1. A photogenic combination—Trumpet Chanterelles on a sphagnum hummock draped with ripe bog cranberries (*Vaccinium vitis-idaea*).

B2

Gomphus clavatus   Pig's Ears
Caps purplish tan with wavy margins; undersides wrinkled and purplish. In rings and clusters on ground under a mixture of old-growth white spruce, poplar and birch; middle to late summer. Edible.
(A 661; G 34; L 396; M 86)

C

Wild Mushroom Cultivation

The cultivation of wild mushrooms has long held peoples' imaginations. Today it could be properly termed a growth hobby and industry. Secrets for growing new varieties are being learned, and several new kinds have appeared recently in grocery supermarkets. Greatest success has been met with species that grow on dead organic matter; species that depend in the wild on symbiotic relationships with trees or other plants are not easily grown in captivity. Who were the first cultivators of wild mushrooms? Probably those people who first discovered that the Oyster Mushroom (*Pleurotus ostreatus*), 48G and p.93, can be stimulated to sprout by watering "oyster logs" lugged home from the forest.

(For further reading: articles in *Mushroom, the Journal of Wild Mushrooming*, 861 Harold St., Moscow, Idaho, U.S.A., 83843.)

Ridged Fungi

A

B1

B2

C

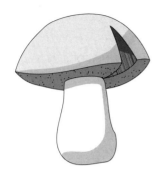

Fleshy Pored Fungi
(Undersurfaces of fleshy caps have a soft sponge-like layer of tubes)

Family Boletaceae   The Boletes

Beginning mushroomers soon become acquainted with this large family of soft-tubed mushrooms. It is often necessary to examine the undersurface of the cap to make sure it is a Bolete and not a gilled mushroom. All Boletes have mycorrhizal relationships.
(A 488; G 220; L 562; M 100; S 194)

Cross section of a *Leccinum* showing the sponge-like layers of tubes, a property of the family Boletaceae. The exposed flesh is beginning to stain purple, a useful feature for differentiating species of *Leccinum*.

Forest renewal. A spruce seedling that sprouted on a decomposed spruce stump. Earlier in spring this stump displayed a large cluster of *Mycena overholtzii* (Snowbank Fairy Helmet), 48C. It is not unusual to see spruce seedlings on stumps and logs that have been decomposed by saprophytic fungi.

A

Genus *Boletus*

This is a large genus that receives extensive coverage in most field guides, but it has few representatives in the northern forest.
(A 511; M 103; S 194)

Boletus edulis   King Bolete
Warm brown caps; massive stalks marked with fine net-like ridges. Considered by many in North America and Europe to be the "king" of edible mushrooms, but insect larvae often take first claim. May be found under mixed willow, poplar, jack pine and white spruce; July and August. Two of its close neighbours were the next bolete, *Boletus piperatus*, and *Amanita muscaria*, 4B. Edible.
    (A 530, G 224; L 568; M 104; S 195)

Boletus piperatus   Peppery Bolete
Cap and pore surface both showing red; base of stalk yellow with attached bright yellow mycelium. Under willow and poplar in jack pine forest; midsummer. Edible with caution because of possible ill effects.
(A 517; G 230; L 571; M 108; S 196)

B

C

Wild Mushrooms in the Provincial Economy

There is a strong demand on the world market for wild mushrooms from the boreal forest. In 1996 over 200 persons earned income from harvesting wild mushrooms in Northern Saskatchewan. Pickers sell to buyers who in turn fill North American and overseas orders. Three kinds of mushrooms account for the bulk of the commercial harvest:

- Morel (*Morchella* spp.), 78C. Much of the Morel crop is dried before sale.
- Golden Chanterelle (*Cantharellus cibarius*), 54A. Most of Saskatchewan's harvest of Chanterelle goes to Germany. Approximately 66,000 pounds of Chanterelle, valued at $264,000 to pickers, were harvested in Northern Saskatchewan in 1996.
- Matsutake or Pine Mushroom (*Tricholoma magnivelare*), 50F. Major demand for Pine Mushroom is from Japan.

Information courtesy of:
Gerry Ivanochko, Saskatchewan Agriculture and Food
Del Phillips, Saskatchewan Environment and Resource Management

Fleshy Pored Fungi

A

B

C

Genus *Fuscoboletinus*

A genus of colder habitats, well represented in the northern forest but not given thorough coverage in most field guides with a more southern focus. Large angular pores, often radially arranged, help to identify members.
(A 505; S 202)

Fuscoboletinus aeruginascens   Greyish Larch
  (or *F. serotinus*?)   Bolete
Greyish cap; off-white pores; slight bluish-green staining when bruised. An attractive species but chocolate-brown slime over the cap discourages handling. Tamarack and black spruce bogs, late summer. Edible.
(A 507)

A

Fuscoboletinus spectabilis   Admirable Bolete
Cap reddish with grey patches; pore surface yellow; red, gelatinous veil between cap edge and stalk that collapses on stalk. There are few more striking mushrooms than this species in its prime. Boggy habitats under tamarack and black spruce; mostly an autumn species, but occasional specimen as early as June. Edible.
(A 506; G 224; S 202)

B

Fuscoboletinus sp.
Not identified beyond genus. Dark, reddish-brown (mahogany), smooth, shiny caps; large, irregular, radially arranged, yellow pores. Isolated groups or colonies at the interface between black spruce/tamarack and jack pine; late summer. Probably edible but not recommended because species uncertain.

C

The Fall Bolete Foursome, from left, *Suillus cavipes* (Hollow-Foot), *Fuscoboletinus spectabilis* (Admirable Bolete), *F. aeruginascens* (Greyish Larch Bolete), *Suillus grevillei* (Tamarack Jack). All four species mycorrhizal with tamarack (larch); sometimes all seen on same outing.

D

Genus *Leccinum*   Roughstems

A stately genus that begs attention in the forest. The dark scales (called scabers) on the usually tall stalks and the colourful caps—oranges, reds, browns, whites—are distinguishing features. Unfortunately, positive recognition at the species level in the field is made difficult in some cases by inconsistent and overlapping cap colourations, somewhat reminiscent of the Russulas. Another interesting property of the genus is the colour changes that occur in the flesh of the cap and stalk of some species when cut—from white to pink, grey or blue. These color changes may help the careful observer to distinguish among similar species of Leccinums.
(A 536; M 111; S 200)

Mushrooms and mycelia that mysteriously glow in the dark are the basis for much of ancient myth and folklore. Stumps in the forest infected with the honey fungus (*Armillaria mellea*), 34A, produce an eerie glow on dark fall nights. Luminous wood was considered a potent source of magic in ancient times.

A

B

C

D

Fleshy Pored Fungi

Feather Moss

A title generally applied to several mosses that frequently carpet the ground under spruce and jack pine (see 12E, 48D). Common names for different species of feather moss include knight's plume and stair-step moss. Feather mosses in the boreal forest abound with mushrooms. Some of these mushrooms arise from mycelia growing in the moss, others from mycelia in substrates under the moss.

Leccinum insigne   Aspen Rough Stem
Reddish-orange to blackish scabers on off-white stalk. Orange- and red-capped Leccinums under poplar during midsummer can be common to abundant and go by the local names "red caps" and "red tops." All red- and orange-capped Leccinums are probably not *L. insigne* since there seem to be seasonal variations in fruiting and some occur in pure stands of jack pine. A good nominee for a provincial mushroom emblem. Edible, see recipe section, pp.92-96.
(A 540; L 578; M 111; S 202)

A

Leccinum scabrum   Birch Bolete
Brown-capped Leccinum with a mycorrhizal relationship with white birch; brown to blackish scabers on whitish stalk. Except during droughty spells, this species can be expected under live birch from early to late summer. When a birch stand dies, this species disappears from underneath. Edible.
(A 541; G 227; L 578; M 111; S 200)

B

Leccinum sp.
Distinctive reddish-brown cap; possibly a different species from *L. insigne*. Widely scattered in thick moss under jack pine; summer. Edible with caution; species uncertain. Sorting out the various species of Leccinums calls for microscopic study along with careful noting of colour changes on wounded flesh.

C

Under jack pine, in background *Monotropa uniflora* (Indian-pipe); in foreground a Leccinum, two Russulas and a Suillus. Indian-pipe is a ghostly parasitic plant that gets its nutrients from the roots of other plants in association with mycorrhizal fungi, possibly the species of fungi shown here that were growing within 5 meters of the Indian-pipe.

Genus *Suillus*   Slippery Jacks

Jack pine is to this genus what poplar and birch are to *Leccinum*. *Suillus* is also found with spruce and tamarack. The "slippery" connotation applies to those species that are sticky or slimy when moist; some species of *Suillus* in the northern forest have dry caps.
(A 491; M 113; S 196)

Suillus brevipes   Short-Stemmed Slippery Jack
Brown cap, sticky when moist; stalk white and spotless; bruised flesh not turning blue. Early to late summer; under jack pine. Edible.
(A 501; G 229; L 582; M 114; S 200)

D

Suillus cavipes   Hollow-Foot
Dry, densely woolly caps, usually reddish brown rarely yellow; ring on stalk; lower portion of stalk hollow; large, angular, yellow pores. Scattered and in groups; some years very common, others rare; late season. Associated with tamarack, sometimes in presence of spruce and jack pine. Edible.
(A 494, G 223; L 583; M 114; S 198)

E

A

B

C

Environmental Impact

Does picking mushrooms harm the fungus or the environment? It is often likened to picking apples; in both cases the growing structures are not affected. Providing the mycelium and substrate are not impaired, and some of each species are left intact to spread spores and as food for wild animals, picking the mushrooms appears to be harmless. Species and localities may vary in their responses to picking, and picking should never be done carelessly or in excess.

D

E

Suillus granulatus   Dotted Slippery Jack
Brown cap, may appear streaky or mottled, sticky when moist; stalk covered with small reddish dots. Summer; under jack pine. Edible.
(A 502; G 229; L 584; M 115; S 199)

A

Suillus grevillei   Tamarack Jack
Reddish-brown to golden cap, smooth and shiny, slimy in wet weather; prominent ring on stalk; pore surface slowly bruises reddish brown. A late-season bolete associated with bogs and tamarack, sometimes in company with spruce and jack pine. Edible. This is one of four impressive bog species (others: *S. cavipes, Fuscoboletinus aeruginascens, F. spectabilis*) that have been given the collective title, The Fall Bolete Foursome, 58D.
(A 497; G 229; L 584; M 117; S 198)

B

Suillus tomentosus Blue-Staining Slippery Jack
Prime caps orange-yellow covered with dry, fuzzy, brownish scales that may disappear; flesh when broken and pore surface when rubbed turn blue, sometimes slowly. Common in summer under jack pine. Edible.
(A 504; L 590; M 119; S 199)

C

Suillus umbonatus   Peaked Suillus
Mottled, greenish-brown, knobbed cap; gelatinous ring on stalk; large angular pores. In large groups in mossy areas under jack pine; uncommon during study; late summer. Edible but poorly rated.
(A 498; M 120; S 196)

D

Toothed Fungi
(Undersurfaces of caps have teeth or spines)

Family Hydnaceae
This is a large and diverse group of forest mushrooms that produce their spores on teeth or spines. It often comes as a surprise to turn over the cap of a mushroom and see something other than gills or pores. Several toothed mushrooms are highly distinctive and can be readily identified in the field. This group does well in the boreal forest. Some authors divide the toothed fungi into several families.
(A 611; G 240; L 426; M 87; S 368)

A

B

C

D

Toothed Fungi

Myco-

Beginning mushroomers often hear and are puzzled by words beginning with "myco." Translate that to "mushroom" or "fungus" and arrive at the following meanings:

Mycology: A branch of science dealing with fungi

Mycologist: A fungal specialist

Mycologize: To study fungi

Mycorrhiza: A symbiotic association of the mycelium of a fungus
                with the roots of a seed plant

Mycophagy: The eating of mushrooms

Mycophagist: A person who eats mushrooms

Mycophile: A person who loves mushrooms

Mycophobe: A person who fears mushrooms

Mycophilatelist: A collector of mushroom postage stamps

Genus *Auriscalpium*

Auriscalpium vulgare   Ear Pick Fungus
Small, brown, hairy cap; stalk usually attached to side of cap. An attractive oddity among forest fungi. Small size and dark colours make it difficult to spot but it is more conspicuous under moist conditions when the shriveled cap fully expands. Usually singly but sometimes in groups; in jack pine and spruce forests, on decaying cones, twigs and other debris. Inedible.
(A 629; L 426; M 87; S 369)

A1

Same species as A1. Two specimens growing from a fallen pine cone. Toothed underside of cap seen on left. This dainty, inconspicuous, fascinating mushroom is often spotted first by sharp-eyed children.

A2

Genus *Dentinum*

Dentinum repandum   Hedgehog Mushroom
(Also known as *Hydnum repandum*)
Cap yellow-orange, smooth, irregular; the top of the cap may suggest a gilled mushroom but the bottom says otherwise. Terrestrial in various wooded habitats; summer and fall. Edible, see recipe section, pp.92-96.
(A 618; G 241; L 428; M 89; S 368)

B

Genus *Hericium*

Hericium ramosum   Comb Tooth
Fruiting body white, much branched, covered with hanging teeth. A leading candidate for most strikingly beautiful and distinctive mushroom in the northern forest. When it blooms in all its glory, it brightens up the dark forest floor. On fallen, decomposing poplar logs; summer. Edible, see recipe section, pp.92-96.
(A 615; L 431; M 92; S 370)

C

Genus *Hydnellum*

Hydnellum caeruleum   Bluish Hydnellum
Bluish tones. Thick, tough, woody caps, tinged blue near the margin; undersurface with short teeth, tinged blue when young. Photographed under spruce in September. Inedible.
(A 625; L 432; M 93; S 366)

D

Hydnellum pineticola   Pine Hydnellum
Pinkish tones; flesh in caps and stalks tough and woody, often with imbedded debris; easy to recognize when covered with pink droplets. Forest floor under jack pine; midsummer. Inedible.
(A 627; L 434; S 366)

E

Genus *Hydnum* (*Sarcodon* for some authors)

This genus among the toothed fungi is highly distinctive: mostly large, dark, coarse caps covered with spines, scales and/or cracks; flesh thick and firm but not woody; teeth usually dark. The genus contains several species that often defy accurate identification in the field.
(A 616; M 95; S 367)

A1

A2

B

C

D

E

Food Value of Wild Mushrooms

Cooks as a rule seek the unique flavours of wild mushrooms and are less concerned about nutritional value. But wild mushrooms add more than flavouring; they also contain useful amounts of various vitamins, minerals, and trace elements. Authors generally rank the food value of mushrooms on a par with most vegetables.

Hydnum fuscoindicum   Violet Hedgehog
Coarse caps purple to black; flesh deep purple.
Widely scattered groups under spruce; summer.
Inedible. Species identification uncertain; there
are confusing look-alikes.
(A 622)

A

Hydnum imbricatum   Shingled Hedgehog
Cap like a large, brown macaroon; cap scales
pronounced; flesh greyish to dark brown; stalk
base dark brown, not showing olive or green.
Common some years under spruce and jack
pine; summer and fall. Edible but not
recommended because of possible confusion
with other species.
(A 619; L 434; M 96; S 368)

B1

Same species as B1 or a similar species. In
feather moss under open jack pine; autumn.
Widely scattered but large size and light colour
often make several visible from any place where
you may be standing in the forest. These two
growing together resemble a large tortoise.

B2

Hydnum scabrosum   Bitter Hedgehog
Resembles *H. imbricatum* but the caps of Bitter
Hedgehog are smaller and less scaly and the
stalk base is olive or bluish green. Under jack
pine and spruce; midsummer and later. Inedible,
distasteful.
(A 620; L 435; M 95; S 367)

C

Genus *Phellodon*

Phellodon tomentosus   Zoned Phellodon
Caps zoned in shades of brown with white
margins; caps often fused to form clusters; teeth
minute, white. In moss under jack pine, late
summer and fall. Edibility unknown.
(A 628; L 436; M 98; S 364)

D

When I saw these strange eyes staring up from
the forest floor, forest gnomes came to mind.
The inverted, miniature caps with greyish
centres are growing from the top of a Russula.

A

B1

B2

C

D

When Do Mushrooms Bloom?

Apart from the obvious role of moisture, trying to predict or fully explain when fungi bloom challenges the most experienced observers. Many mushrooms in central Saskatchewan are on different schedules than reported in some field guides. For example, several of the same species bloom in summer around Prince Albert and in fall, winter and spring in California (Arora 1986). Then, too, some species skip a year or more or alternate good crops with poor. More factors than just weather conditions seem to be at work.

Coral and Club Fungi
(Bodies coral-like or club shaped)

Family Clavariaceae

These fungi do not fit most popular perceptions of what mushrooms should look like. Instead of the typical cap-and-stalk shape, these mushrooms resemble erect clubs and branched corals. They are a fascinating group but not one that is easily mastered at the species level. All are saprophytic on the forest floor or on wood. Some authors split this group into additional families.
(A 630; G 242; L 398; M 70; S 360)

Genus *Clavariadelphus*

Clavariadelphus borealis   Northern Pestle
Body is orange to orange brown, club shaped and flattened on top. In moss beds under spruce and jack pine; summer. Not common. Edible.
(A 634; L 404; M 72; S 361)

A

Clavariadelphus sachalinensis   Strap-Shaped Pestle
Yellowish, slender, club-shaped bodies. Sometimes abundant, in troops, on humus under jack pine and spruce; summer. Edible. Among many interesting sidelights in Schalkwijk-Barendsen (1991) is that this species is named after the Russian island of Sakhalin where it was discovered by Japanese mycologists in the thirties.
(A 633; L 403; M 73; S 361)

B

Genus *Clavicorona*

Clavicorona pyxidata   Crowned Coral
Numerous tiered, pale yellow branches with crown-like tips (use hand lens for better view). One of few corals that grow on wood—most corals are found on ground in duff. Very impressive when seen in prime condition on rotting poplar and birch logs. May appear in early summer. Edible.
(A 642; L 401; M 73; S 362)

C

Genus *Macrotyphula*

Macrotyphula juncea   Fairy Hair
Questionable identity at species level; not well-covered in references. Thin and hairlike. Abundant and striking on rotting poplar leaves and twigs following late summer and fall rains, often in company with White Pinwheel (*Marasmius epiphyllus*), 44B. Edibility unknown.
(A 636)

D

Rare and Endangered Mushrooms

With all the interest being shown rare and endangered birds, mammals and plants, it comes as no surprise when this subject arises during discussions of mushrooms. Some species of mushrooms are encountered only rarely, but none so far has been declared endangered in Canada due to loss of habitat, pollution or other decimating factors. In Europe, several mycorrhizal species have become greatly reduced in quantity and distribution due, it is suspected, to air pollution. Closer to home, a recent newspaper headline "Rare Mushroom Halts Logging" refers to the species *Tricholoma apium* in a small patch of forest northwest of Vancouver. An environmentalist is quoted as saying: "This seems to be the first political mushroom in North America." (*The StarPhoenix*, Saskatoon, May 25, 1996.)

A

B

C

D

Genus *Ramaria*

Ramaria abietina   Green-Staining Coral
Green staining toward base separates this common yellowish species from other branched corals. Under spruce on needle duff; summer. Edible but not recommended because of poor texture and flavour.
(A 650; S 363)

A

Ramaria stricta   Straight Coral
Compact, stately coral; orangish yellow. Late summer on wood in mixed forest. Edible but not recommended because of poor texture and flavour.
(A 648; G 244; L 409; M 74; S 363)

B

Genus *Thelephora*

Ramaria sp.   Orange-Red Coral
A striking, but locally uncommon mushroom. Exact species not determined. When first spotted at a distance, it may resemble a piece of discarded orange-red flagging tape. In rich leaf duff under mixed spruce, willow, poplar and birch following heavy rains of early August. Edibility unknown.

C

Thelephora terrestris   Earth Fan
Questionable identity at species level; can be confused with look-alikes. Vase-shaped, brown, fibrous caps; undersurface smooth with radiating wrinkles. On ground in several habitats; summer. Inedible.
(A 608; L 413; M 78; S 365)

D

Woody Pored Fungi
(Undersurfaces of tough caps have a layer of tubes)

Family Polyporaceae   The Woody Polypores

Mostly woody and leathery species that are found on logs, stumps and living and dead trees. The boletes also are pored fungi but are fleshy and terrestrial. Woody polypores come in a wide variety of shapes, e.g., hoof-like, bracket-like, shelf-like; some are perennial, adding a new layer of tubes each growing season. Several species are easily identified, others baffle even advanced students. Visit a dead and dying stand of white birch for a quick introduction to woody polypores. (A 549; G 237; L 439; M 125; S 371)

A

B

C

D

Scientific Names

The language of mushrooms, to the displeasure of many beginners, still communicates with names in Latin and Greek. This will be the case until common names become standardized as they have for birds and flowering plants. For all their lack of appeal, scientific names have special fascination: many are easily translated while others contain imaginative descriptions. Witness the following:

Boletus "edulis":	edible
Pholiota "destruens":	destroying
Boletus " piperatus":	peppery
Agaricus "haemorrhoidarius":	bleeding
Suillus "brevipes":	short stalked
"Coprinus" spp.:	dung
Suillus "cavipes":	hollow foot
Amanita "muscaria":	having to do with flies
Clavariadelphus "borealis":	northern
Cortinarius "trivialis":	common
Fuscoboletinus "spectabilis":	remarkable
"Lycoperdon" spp.:	wolf fart

Genus *Albatrellus*

Albatrellus ovinus Sheep Polypore
An exception among the woody polypores, resembling a bolete in several respects: it grows on the ground; has a cap, pores and stalk; is not woody. However, its shape is often irregular, the flesh is thick and firm, and the tube layer is tough and adheres tightly to the cap. Colour is off-white, usually with a tinge of lemon yellow, green or orange. Under jack pine; colonial but not common; late summer. Inedible.
(A 557; G 239; L 444)

A

Genus *Bjerkandera*

Bjerkandera adusta Smoky Polypore
Smoky-grey caps, whitish margins when young; shelf-like in overlapping layers on poplar stumps and logs; pore surface grey or black; pores minute. The colour of the pore surface and the size of the pores help to distinguish this species from several others. Inedible.
(A 596; L 445)

B

Genus *Coltricia*

Coltricia cinnamomea Fairy Stool
Thin, concentrically zoned, brownish cap on a tough, brown, velvety stalk. An attractive terrestrial polypore found along trails and in moss under jack pine. Annual, often alongside last year's dull-coloured caps. Inedible. Identification at level of species open to question.
(A 568; L 450)

C

Genus *Fomes*

Fomes fomentarius Tinder Conk
Grey; woody; perennial; hoof-shaped. Found on dead hardwoods, especially birch. Used down through the years as tinder for starting fires. Inedible.
(A 581; L 457; S 374)

D

Genus *Fomitopsis*

Fomitopsis pinicola Red-Belted Conk
Woody, knob-shaped and cream coloured when young; shelf-like with red zones on surface with age; white to yellow pores. Perennial on spruce stumps and logs. A major decomposer of dead spruce. Inedible.
(A 578; L 459; M 126)

E

Genus *Ganoderma*

Ganoderma applanatum Artist's Conk
Cap grey to brown, woody, shelf-like; pore surface white, bruising brown; brown spores often coating caps and adjacent surfaces. Perennial; common at the base of dying and dead poplars. Inedible.
(A 576; L 460; M 127; S 377)

F

Genus *Inonotus*

Inonotus tomentosus Woolly Velvet Polypore
Questionable identity at species level; possible confusion with similar appearing species. Yellowish-brown cap; brownish pore surface; short stalk. Pictured specimens are growing on ground from shallowly buried spruce roots; also under jack pine; late summer. Inedible. The green leaves are incorporated into the specimen on the right.
(A 569; L 471)

G

Genus *Lenzites*

Lenzites betulina Gilled Polypore
Cap leathery to woody; upper surface multicoloured, velvety and zoned. Another exception among woody polypores—there are gills on the undersurface of the cap. On dead birch and other hardwoods; annual, but dead bodies overwinter. Inedible.
(A 589; L 469; M 128; S 375)

H

Woody Pored Fungi

74

Genus *Phellinus*

Phellinus tremulae   False Tinder Conk
Woody, blackish, cracked cap; perennial; pore surface often tilted upwards. Parasitic; occurs up and down the trunks of live, older white poplar trees, emerging immediately below dead branches. Inedible.
(A 581)

A

Genus *Piptoporus*

Piptoporus betulinus   Birch Conk
Very distinctive polypore: margin on cap thick, blunt, inrolled, resembling a curb; only on birch both living and dead, mostly the latter. Annual, but caps overwinter and slowly deteriorate. Reported as edible when young. Has been used as a polishing ingredient, an anesthetic, and for mounting insect specimens
(A 584; G 238; L 477; S 374)

B

Genus *Polyporus*

Polyporus badius   Black-Leg
Thin, leatherlike, reddish-brown caps on poplar logs; can grow large—20 cm or more in diameter. Specimens become rigid in age and may overwinter. Inedible.
(A 562; L 478)

C

Genus *Schizophyllum*

Schizophyllum commune   Split-Gill
Fan-shaped, greyish-white, hairy caps; unique, lengthwise split gills that fold back in dry weather. On decaying poplar; all season long. Inedible. (An odd fungus; because of its texture and shape, treated here as a polypore.)
(A 590; G 164; L 493; M 80; S 364)

D

Genus *Trichaptum*

Trichaptum biformis   Violet-Pored Bracket Fungus
Tough, thin, overlapping caps; pore surface violet tinged. Common on fallen poplar logs; massive fruitings can be quite spectacular when they cover a large log. Inedible.
(A 593; L 490)

E

Cross section of a Tinder Conk (*Fomes fomentarius*), 72D, a perennial polypore, showing annual layers of woody tubes.

A

B

C

D

E

Woody Pored Fungi

More Scientific Names . . .

Clitocybe "maxima":	the biggest
Otidea "onotica":	of the donkey
Collybia "acervata":	bundled
"Spathularia" flavida:	like a spatula
Nolanea "mammosa":	with a nipple
Agaricus "silvicola":	forest dweller

(continued from p. 71)

Puffballs and Earthstars

Family Geastraceae

Geastrum is the only genus in this family.
(A 699; M 359; S 349)

Genus *Geastrum*   Earthstars

Earthstars are puffballs with rays. The rays form as the outer wall of the fungus splits and curls back and under during growth. The ball-like centre is known as the spore case. Spores are disseminated through an apical pore in the spore case. The slightest pressure on the spore case, even from rain drops, causes spores to be released. Earthstars are unmistakable as to genus but the several species are not so easily differentiated. Annual, but last year's specimens are commonly found in the spring; saprophytic.
(A 699; L 816; M 359; S 349)

Geastrum pectinatum (on left) Beaked Earthstar
(*G. sessile*, centre)
(*G. quadrifidum*, right)
G. pectinatum has spore case mounted on a very thin stalk (pedicel); apical pore is beak-like; usually more than four rays. In groups in needle litter under spruce. Inedible but ornamental. Pictured are dried specimens.
(A 702; L 818; M 360; S 350)

A

Geastrum quadrifidum   Four-Pointed Earthstar
Stands on 4-5 rays; pore of spore case encircled with a pale ring or halo. In groups under spruce. Inedible. Pictured are dried specimens.
(A 702; S 349)

B

Geastrum sessile   Fringed Earthstar
Usually six or more rays; with fringed tissue around the pore mouth (no beak or halo). Grouped in needle duff under spruce. Inedible. Pictured are fresh specimens.
(A 704; S 350)

C

The larger conk attached to the birch log was facing downward when the log was standing upright (see 73D). Then when the log fell the now prostrate conk responded by producing a new, properly oriented cap on its own pore surface. The tubes in the cap must be vertical (facing downwards) in order for spores to be released.

More Scientific Names . . .

Tricholoma "saponaceum":	resembling soap
"Dentinum" repandum:	possessing teeth
Limacella "glioderma":	with gluey skin
Armillaria "mellea":	honey coloured
Paxillus "vernalis":	of the spring
Geastrum "quadrifidum":	divided in four
"Lactarius deliciosus":	delicious milkcap
Hydnellum "pineticola":	pine forest dweller
Camarophyllus "pratensis":	growing in meadows
Clitocybe "odora":	fragrant
Albatrellus "ovinus":	pertaining to sheep
Russula "nigricans":	blackening
Polyporus "badius":	reddish brown
Hygrophorus "piceae":	of spruce
Galerina "autumnalis":	belonging to autumn

(continued from p. 75)

Puffballs and Earthstars

A

B

C

Family Lycoperdaceae

There are several genera of puffballs (some species are as large or larger than basketballs and weigh many pounds) but only small, woodland varieties (genus *Lycoperdon*) are common in the boreal forest.
(A 690; M 350; S 344)

Genus *Lycoperdon*   Puffballs

Woodland puffballs are small—like earthstars but without rays. The genus, *Lycoperdon*, is distinctive but its several forest species can be confusing. Old, dull-coloured, deflated specimens are a common sight on the forest floor after snow melts in the spring. Puffballs are saprophytic.
(A 690; L 816; M 354; S 344)

Lycoperdon perlatum   Common Puffball
Spore cases white and spiny when young but spines often disappear; brown spores puff from mouths of mature specimens. Scattered or bunched on the forest floor in several woodland habitats. Edible when young but do not confuse it with the egg stage of deadly Amanitas. An Amanita "egg" when sliced in half vertically reveals a preformed mushroom; no mushroom shape is seen inside a puffball.
(A 693; G 252; L 825; M 355; S 346)

 A

Lycoperdon pyriforme   Pear-Shaped Puffball
Pear-shaped, smooth, brownish spore cases. A late-summer forest spectacle when thickly clustered on rotting logs. Root-like threads of white mycelia (called rhizomorphs) penetrate the decomposing substrate. Edible when young but do not confuse it with the egg stage of deadly Amanitas.
(A 691; G 252; L 826; M 356; S 346)

 B

Morels
(Caps pitted or wrinkled)

Family Morchellaceae
A family famous for its tasty, springtime morels.
(A 784; L 326; M 36; S 344)

Genus *Morchella*

Morchella elata   Black Morel
Dark, conical, pitted cap; margin of cap attached to stalk—not free as on *Verpa*. Spring and early summer; under a variety of trees but mainly poplar and jack pine; common in some years, scarce in others. Recently burned jack pine forests are especially renowned for morels. Edible, see recipe section, pp.92-96. *Morchella esculenta* is similar except for its yellowish colour and sponge-like shape of its pits.
(A 790; G 258; L 326; M 39; S 381)

C1

A famous duo, *Morchella elata* and *M. esculenta*, Black and Yellow Morels. This "mixed bag" was gathered in the same stand of open poplar in late May. The Yellow Morel is the official mushroom emblem of the state of Minnesota.

C2

Chemical Analysis

Mushroom identification can be advanced by the use of chemicals; two in particular, potassium hydroxide (KOH) and Melzer's reagent, an iodine solution. KOH has no visible effect on some mushrooms, while staining others different colours, such as yellow, green, and brown. Melzer's reagent has no visible effect on some white to yellow spore prints, but causes others to turn blue-black and still others reddish brown.

A

B

Microscopic Analysis

A microscope can be a tremendous aid in mushroom identification. Spores of different groups and species when magnified show different sizes, shapes and surface features. The microscope also reveals the presence or absence of certain cells in parts of the mushroom and differences in gill tissues among species.

C1

C2

Morels

Genus *Verpa*

Verpa bohemica — Wrinkled Thimble Cap
Wrinkled or furrowed thimble-shaped cap; cap attached only at top of stalk; sides of cap hang down skirt-like. A spring beauty soon after forest reawakens in May; on forest floor under poplar and willow. Edible with caution because of possible ill effects.
(A 793; G 258; L 329; M 42; S 380)

A

Verpa conica — Smooth Thimble Cap
Smooth, brown, thimble-like cap attached only at apex of stalk. Solitary or at times in groups; mostly on moist soil at edge of springtime ponds in mixed forest; early summer. Not as common as *Verpa bohemica* (Wrinkled Thimble Cap). Edible following cooking.
(A 794; G 259; L 329; M 43; S 380)

B

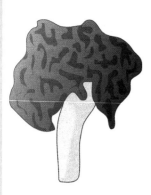

False Morels and Elfin Saddles
(Members of this group may be cup-like, saucer-like, brain-like or saddle-shaped)

Family Helvellaceae
This is the only family in this category of mushrooms. Members of three genera are shown.
(A 796; L 326; M 43; S 382)

Genus *Discina*

Discina perlata — Pig's Ears
Brown, cup-like or ear-shaped; usually with a stubby, ribbed stalk. Early spring; on ground and on and around old stumps under spruce. The season and habitat are usually reliable indicators of this species, but doubts arise over exact identities when other cup-shaped mushrooms are seen a bit later in other habitats. Edible but not recommended because of possible confusion with other cup-shaped species.
(A 798; L 331; M 47)

C

Genus *Gyromitra*

Gyromitra esculenta — False Morel or Brain Mushroom
An impressive brownish fungus; large specimens resemble a grapefruit-sized brain. May/June; scattered under jack pine often in beds of reindeer moss (lichen); common some springs, rare others. Deadly poisonous but eaten by some people in some parts of the world with no apparent ill effects. Method of preparation may be the key. (See p.33).
(A 801; G 259; L 336; M 51; S 382)

D

A

B

The Canadian Tuckahoe

This was a much-discussed subject during pioneering times across the poplar grove and forest region of the prairie provinces. Farmers would unearth black, rubbery bodies, the size of apples and larger, while clearing and breaking poplar-covered lands. Children in turn would bring these oddities to school, and teachers would send the specimens away for identification. They turned out to be the resting stage of the fungus *Polyporus tuberaster*, which sends out a colourful mushroom in some summers. It was mistakenly thought that the rubbery bodies were pemmican or dried buffalo meat, remnants of the earlier pre-settlement period. The species is not commonly reported today.

(Reference: *The Canadian Tuckahoe*. 1952. T. C. Vanterpool. *The Blue Jay*, Volume 10.)

C

D

False Morels and Elfin Saddles

Gyromitra infula   Hooded False Morel
Distinctive saddle-shaped, brownish cap; sturdy, whitish stalk. Late summer; on ground or rotten wood; several habitats. Poisonous.
(A 802; G 260; L 339; M 53; S 382)

A

Helvella acetabulum   Ribbed Elfin Cup
Brown cup mushroom with clasping white ribs; stubby stalk. Summer; on ground; several forest habitats. Edibility unknown.
(A 807; L 332; M 43)

B

Helvella crispa   Fluted White Elfin Saddle
Robust fruiting body; white, irregular head; tall, white, fluted stalk. Late summer on moss under spruce. A distinctive and beautiful species; like a fancy white candle in a darkened forest. Reported as edible but not recommended because of possible ill effects.
(A 816, G 260; L 333; M 44; S 383)

C

Helvella elastica   Brown Elfin Saddle
A dainty, brown, saddle-shaped cap on a slender white stalk. August; on humus and moss under white spruce. Edibility unknown.
(A 813; G 261; L 334; M 45; S 384)

D

Cup Fungi

(An accepted but misleading term since many cup-shaped fungi are found in other groups and a main member of this group is more ear-than cup-shaped)

Family Pezizaceae

The only family under this heading. Species from two genera are shown.
(A 817; L 326; M 55; S 384)

A

B

C

D

Cup Fungi

Mushroom Classification

Fungi are classified scientifically on the basis of their similarities and differences. At the bottom of the scale is the species—individuals that have a unique set of properties and that breed true through generations. Closely related species are grouped in a genus, genera in a family, families in an order, and so on until the highest level, Kingdom Fungi, is reached.

Scientists at the close of the 20th Century are still uncertain about the correct classification of many fungi. It is no easy task in the first place to settle on what is or is not a separate species and, in the second place, to decide where a species belongs on the classification ladder. Scientists are continually reworking older names and classifications while at the same time discovering new species. Non-professional mushroomers should not allow these important but confusing scientific activities to spoil their fun.

Genus *Otidea*

Otidea onotica　　　　　　　　Donkey Ears
Erect ear-like fruiting body. The common name
says it all! Scattered and gregarious on ground
under spruce; summer. Reported as edible but
not recommended because of possible ill effects.
(A 832; L 352; S 387)

A

Genus *Peziza*

Peziza repanda　　　　　　　　Brown Cup
Thin, fragile flesh; stalkless or virtually so.
Found most often on decaying poplar logs or
buried wood in mixed forest; summer. A
common species in a large, difficult genus.
Reported as edible but not recommended
because of possible confusion with other species
of uncertain edibility.
(A 821; G 261; L 347; S 385)

B

Jelly Fungi
(Mushrooms that have rubbery or gelatinous textures)

Family Corticiaceae
(L 416; M 79)

Genus *Christiansenia*

Christiansenia mycetophila　　　Collybia Jelly
Pale cream-yellow clusters fused to caps and
stalks of *Collybia dryophila*, the June
Mushroom, 38D. The June Mushroom is
common and widespread most years, but
Collybia Jelly is seen infrequently. Edibility
unknown.
(A 216; L 418)

C

Family Dacrymycetaceae
(G 245; L 380; M 64)

Genus *Calocera*

Calocera cornea　　　　Staghorn Jelly Fungus
Very small, erect, yellow, club-like fruiting
bodies; best appreciated through a hand lens. In
groups; along tops of moist poplar logs;
summer. Edibility unknown.
(A 675; L 381; M 65)

D

Family Tremellaceae
(G 245; M 65)

Genus *Exidea*

Exidea glandulosa　　　　　Black Jelly Roll
Irregularly lobed, black, gelatinous bodies
strung out on dead poplar and alder branches.
Early summer; uncommon. Edibility unknown.
(A 672; L 382; M 66)

E

Genus *Phlogiotis*

Phlogiotis helvelloides　Apricot Jelly Mushroom
Fruiting bodies spatula-shaped, rubbery,
translucent, clear to apricot-coloured. Grouped
in duff under mixed spruce and poplar; summer;
not common. Edible.
(A 672; G 246; L 383; M 66)

F

A

B

Starting Out

When *Mushroom, the Journal of Wild Mushrooming* (Box 3156, Moscow, Idaho, U.S.A., 83843) asked experienced mushroomers what advice they would give the beginning mushroom hunter, the top five items were: buy and use good field guides, join a mycological society, take a mushroom identification course, go out with an experienced mushroomer, and keep a journal and make good notes.

Jelly Fungi

C

D

E

F

Genus *Pseudohydnum*

Pseudohydnum gelatinosum   Toothed Jelly Fungus

An attractive forest oddity. Translucent, greyish, tongue-shaped, rubbery caps; underside of caps with small, rubbery teeth. In wet weather on rotting spruce logs and stumps; summer. Edible. "Pseudohydnum" means this species, with its "teeth," is similar to, but not to be confused with, the true Toothed Fungi, Family Hydnaceae.

(A 671; G 245; L 383; M 66)

A

Genus *Tremella*

Tremella foliacea   Brown Witch's Butter

Brown; flabby; gelatinous. Masses on fallen white spruce trunk; summer. Not recommended for eating; identification questionable at level of species.

(A 673; L 384; M 67)

B

Tremella mesenterica   Witch's Butter

Bright orange; brain-like lobes. On dead spruce and poplar sticks and logs; summer. (Although specimens on both spruce and poplar appear to be identical, the ones on spruce may be a different species, *Dacrymyces palmatus*, Orange Jelly.) Edible.

(A 673; G 246; L 385; M 67)

C

South gate Prince Albert National Park, Saskatchewan, in late September. Poplars showing fall colours; mature jack pine in background.

Other Fungi
(Distinctive forest fungi that are not normally placed in any of the earlier groups)

Genus *Bisporella*

Bisporella citrina   Yellow Fairy Cups

Bright yellow; each cup is minute but they create a striking body when clustered on the side of a wet, barkless poplar log. Summer and fall. Edibility unknown.

(A 877; L 362; S 393)

D

Genus *Chlorociboria*

Chlorociboria aeruginascens   Green Cups

Small, green, cup- or disc-shaped bodies. Not always conspicuous; more noticeable on the forest floor is the blue-green rotten wood on which the Green Cups are formed. The attractively coloured wood is caused by a pigment produced by the mycelium of this fungus. Edibility unknown.

(A 878; L 361; S 393)

E

A

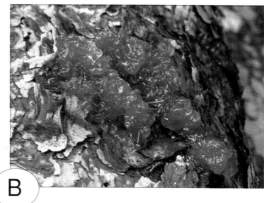

B

C

Other Fungi

Field Notes

The serious mushroomer will want to record the following basic information in the field for identification purposes and future reference: date, location, moisture conditions, habitat, substrate, growth habit and detailed description of each specimen down to and including the mycelium. Final identification may have to be delayed until the specimens are studied more thoroughly at home.

D

E

Genus *Cudonia*

Cudonia circinans   Common Cudonia
Convoluted and droopy cap, cream to buff
coloured. Grouped in moss under spruce;
summer. Poisonous.
(A 873; L 364)

A

Genus *Hypomyces*

Hypomyces luteovirens   Yellow-Green
                                     Hypomyces
A powdery, parasitic fungus that coats the
surfaces of other species, mainly members of
Russula and *Lactarius* (both specimens in the
picture are of same species of *Russula*.).
Occasionally common under moist conditions.
Edibility unknown. Other species and other
colours also occur.
(A 884; L 373; M 30; S 396)

B

Genus *Rhizopogon*

Rhizopogon sp.   False Truffle
Small, potato-like fungi that emerge from sand
under jack pine in late summer and fall;
mycorrhizal. Species uncertain; edibility
unknown. (See p.89).
(A 753; L 813)

C

Genus *Sarcoscypha*

Sarcoscypha hiemalis   Scarlet Elf Cup
Small, orange-scarlet cups. Clustered in leaf
duff on buried twigs. A delightful harbinger of
spring; may appear in early May not far from
remnants of winter's snow. Edibility unknown.
(S 390)

D

Genus *Spathularia*

Spathularia flavida   Fairy Fan
Fruiting body shaped like a canoe paddle;
yellowish. Gregarious under spruce;
occasionally common; summer. Reported to be
a poor edible.
(A 871; L 360; S 392)

E

Late September in Prince Albert National Park,
Saskatchewan. Poplar on left in fall colours;
green forest is a stand of mature white spruce.

Other Fungi

Truffles

The mere mention of truffles (underground fungi) conjures up visions of routing pigs and expensive French cuisine. False truffles (*Rhizopogon* sp.) found in sand under jack pine are not closely related to the true truffles of Europe. False truffles are viewed as inedible, except possibly by squirrels.

Slime Molds

(Not considered to be true fungi but easily mistaken for them)

Genus *Ceratiomyxa*

Ceratiomyxa fruticulosa   Coral Slime
Large, showy, white, creamy masses on moss
and forest debris. Especially common in wet
weather under black spruce; summer. Edibility
unknown.
(L 845)

Genus *Lycogala*

Lycogala epidendrum   Wolf's Milk Slime
Attractive, small, red globules; exude a pink
paste when pressed. Scattered to clustered on
rotting logs, both coniferous and deciduous.
Also called "Toothpaste Slime." Edibility
unknown.
(L 848)

B

Genus *Stemonitis*

Stemonitis splendens   Chocolate Tube Slime
Densely packed, brown, stamen-like, delicate
stalks on rotting logs. One of nature's attractive
oddities; best appreciated through a hand lens.
Inedible.
(L 853)

Edge of boreal forest bog in late September.
Yellowing tamarack backed by black spruce.
Fall boletes were common in this habitat earlier
in month.

Slime Molds

An unsavoury term that has been applied to a group of attractive woodland organisms that never fail to fascinate mushroomers. Some species move about ("flow") and digest nutrients before they alter their appearances and form fruiting bodies. As spore producers they resemble fungi but other features keep them from being classified with the true fungi. Carry and use a hand lens to fully appreciate this unusual group.

A

B

C

The Old and the Bold

It is said there are two kinds of people who gather wild mushrooms for the table: the old and the bold. But beware!, there are no old-bold mushroom pickers.

Mushroom Edibility

Wild mushrooms are intriguing apart from their possible edibility. The fact that some species are choice edibles only adds to the attractiveness of the group as a whole. But anyone who intends to eat wild mushrooms should be aware that there are deadly poisonous species in the northern forest and that timeworn, homespun methods for determining whether or not a species is toxic are not reliable. Obviously, one should proceed with caution before eating a wild mushroom.

The subject of mushroom toxicity is complicated by the fact that several markedly different poisons are involved. It is not a simple matter of only one kind of toxic substance in only one or two species of wild mushrooms. Several species contain different poisons that are deadly to humans, while other species contain various substances that produce harmful but less dreadful effects. Furthermore, certain non-poisonous mushrooms may be inedible for some people because of personal allergies. And who wants to eat a bitter or a woody species just because it is non-poisonous?

Two basic principles should govern the use of wild mushrooms for the table:

1) No mushroom should be eaten until one is absolutely sure of its identity;
2) No mushroom should be eaten until one is absolutely certain it is non-poisonous.

Other precautions you should observe are

1) Use only wholesome, larval-free specimens from pollution-free sites; and,
2) Eat only small amounts at first—cooked, not raw—to test for possible allergic reactions.

In summary, whenever you are considering using wild mushrooms for the table it is always wise to heed the time-honoured warning: "When in doubt, throw it out!"

To be fully appreciated, wild mushrooms require special handling in the kitchen. Simple sautéing does not do all wild species justice. A new mushroomer is fortunate who has a friend who is wise both in the ways of mushroom identification and preparation. Another proven approach to becoming an experienced mushroomer is to participate in organized summer collecting trips, better known as mushroom forays, that have an expert or two in attendance and that include cooking and tasting sessions. Elaborate recipes for preparing wild mushrooms are described in many books on cooking.

This book provides a few simple recipes for five easily identified, non-poisonous species. ***To be safe, none of the other species mentioned in this book as edible should be eaten until you have double-checked the identification with a knowledgeable person or another book.***

Each of the five highlighted species is accompanied by a photograph, detailed description and a suggested method of preparation for the table. Occurrence of the five is spread over the summer, roughly one for each month from May to September, if you are lucky enough to find them: first Black Morels, then Oyster Mushrooms, followed by Aspen Rough Stems, Comb Tooths and Hedgehog Mushrooms. Good mushrooming!

Morchella elata   Black Morels
See also 78C1 and 78C2

Pleurotus ostreatus

Oyster Mushrooms
See also 48G

Leccinum insigne   Aspen Rough Stems
See also 60A

Hericium ramosum   Comb Tooths
See also 64C

Dentinum repandum   Hedgehog Mushrooms
See also 64B

Mushroom Edibility

Morchella elata   Black Morels
Key features:
- Cap dark, cone-shaped and pitted or honey combed; not brain-like or lobed
- Bottom of cap attached to stalk; not free from stalk
- On ground mainly under poplar or jack pine but also scattered in other habitats
- May and into early summer
- Occasional insect damage and infrequent home to ants or snails

Simple Cooking Suggestions: (use either fresh or dried)
- Pick as clean as possible, slice in half vertically
- Sauté fresh morels in olive oil or butter until liquid evaporates
- Serve on crackers or toast

OR
- Crumble dried morels in clear chicken or beef broth and simmer for 10-15 minutes, then serve

Note: To dry morels, place on screen in hot sun or over a dry heat source or in a food dehydrator. When dried to a crisp, store in a sealed container.

Pleurotus ostreatus   Oyster Mushrooms
Key features:
- Undersurface of cap has gills
- Cap smooth, off-white to cream coloured, medium sized to large, shell- or fan-shaped
- Gills white, running down the stalk if a stalk is present
- Stalk present or absent; if present, short, thick, white, off-centre
- Flesh thick, white, tender—not woody
- Spores white
- Occurs in overlapping shelving clusters
- Growing on fallen poplar logs, poplar stumps and dead standing poplar trees mainly in spring and early summer
- Often with small, brown-and-black beetles in the gills

Simple Cooking Suggestions:
- Trim, clean, and save thinner portions of cap that are free of insect damage
- Dip in beaten egg, then dredge in cracker crumbs
- Fry in olive oil or butter until golden brown and serve

Leccinum insigne   Aspen Rough Stems
Key features:
- Undersurface of cap has fleshy tubes and pores in place of gills or teeth
- Cap smooth, colour variable but most recognizable when bright reddish orange
- Stalk whitish covered with reddish to blackish projecting scales
- Flesh thick, white, turning greyish when cut
- Spore print yellow brown
- Scattered or in groups on ground under poplar in summer
- Young specimens less likely to have insect damage
- Similar species, also edible, identified microscopically

Simple Cooking Suggestions: (Expect some darkening of the flesh when cooked)
- Pick clean, avoid washing if possible; further clean with a soft brush
- Discard wormy portions and tube layer if soft
- Slice caps and stems
- Sauté in butter or olive oil until mushrooms are lightly browned
- Serve as a side dish

OR

- After cleaning and slicing caps and stems to equal approximately 2 cups, sauté in 1 tablespoon olive oil or butter with 1 small chopped onion until mushrooms are tender
- Sprinkle with 1 tablespoon flour, 1/4 teaspoon salt and 1/8 teaspoon pepper, and stir to blend
- Add 1/2 cup milk and cook and stir until thickened
- Stir in 1/2 cup sour cream; heat through but do not boil
- Serve on toast or as a side dish

Hericium ramosum   Comb Tooths
Key features:
- No well-defined cap
- Structure white, much branched, covered with hanging teeth
- Spore colour white
- In clumps on rotting poplar logs in summer
- Usually free of insect damage

Simple Cooking Suggestions
- Select young, firm, clean specimens
- Slice and simmer for 5–10 minutes in own moisture until moisture evaporates
- Sauté in olive oil or butter and season lightly with garlic salt
- Serve plain or on toast
- Or add to rice casserole or to chicken or turkey stir-fried dishes

Mushroom Edibility

Dentinum repandum Hedgehog Mushrooms
Key features:
- Undersurface of cap has teeth in place of gills or pores
- Cap yellow orange, smooth, irregular, up to 10 cm across
- Flesh white, soft, thick, usually free of insect damage
- Spores white
- Several habitats, singly or in groups on ground or in moss
- Late summer and fall

Simple Cooking Suggestions:
- Pick clean or further clean with dry mushroom brush
- Slice and sauté in olive oil or butter until liquid evaporates
- Serve plain or on toast
- Also delicious as an addition to scrambled eggs and omelets
- Or use in place of *Leccinum insigne* in the creamed mushroom recipe

Glossary

angular: (of pores), 4- to 6-sided with corners or angles.

apex: top.

apical pore: the spore mouth in certain puffballs and earthstars.

ascus (pl. asci): the cell in which spores of the Ascomycetes are produced.

autodigestion: self-digestion, dissolving into liquid.

basal: at or near the base.

basidium (pl. basidia): the cell on which spores of the Basidiomycetes are formed.

bulbous: stalk with an enlarged base.

button: a young mushroom before it has opened.

close: (of gills), narrowly spaced.

conifer: a cone-bearing tree—spruce, jackpine, tamarack, balsam fir.

conk: a woody polypore.

cortina: the cobwebby or silky veil found in some mushrooms.

cuticle: the surface layer or skin of the cap of a mushroom.

decurrent: (of gills or tubes), descending or running down the stalk.

disc: the central portion of the cap.

distant: (of gills), widely spaced.

duff: litter on the forest floor.

egg: the immature stage of some mushrooms, mainly the Amanitas.

ephemeral: existing only briefly.

evanescent: disappearing.

fairy ring: a circle or arc of mushrooms.

family: a group of related genera.

fibrillose: (of cap or stalk), with thin thread-like filaments.

floccose: cottony to woolly.

forked: (of gills), dividing into two.

free: (of gills), not attached to the stalk.

fruiting body: the reproductive portion of a fungus; a mushroom.

genus (pl. genera): a group of closely related species.

glandular dots: spots or smears on the stalks of certain mushrooms.

glutinous: sticky or slimy.

granulose: covered with granules.

habitat: place of growth.

humus: decaying organic matter in or on soil.

hygrophanous: (of the cap), changing markedly in colour as it dries.

inrolled: incurved or bent inward.

KOH: solution of potassium hydroxide used to test colour reactions.

latex: milky juice found in some mushrooms.

LBM: little brown mushroom.

look-alikes: two or more species that appear to be the same.

macroscopic: visible without a microscope.

margin: the edge of a mushroom cap or gill.

Melzer's reagent: a chemical solution containing iodine used to test colour reactions in mushrooms.

membranous: thin and pliant like a membrane or skin.

microscopic: visible only with a microscope.

middens: heaps of conifer cones and mushrooms gathered by squirrels.

mycelial mat: dense mycelium seen in duff and humus.

mycelium (pl. mycelia): the vegetative part of a fungus.

mycorrhiza (pl. mycorrhizae): a symbiotic association between a fungus and the roots of a plant.

mycorrhizal fungus: a fungus having a mutually beneficial association with the roots of a plant.

parasitic fungus: a fungus that feeds on another living organism.

pedicel: a slender stalk.

pores: the mouths or openings of the tubes of fleshy and woody polypores.

radially arranged: (of pores), in rows like the spokes of a wheel.

reticulate: (of caps and stalks), marked with net-like lines or ridges.

rhizomorph: a cord-like strand of mycelium.

ring: the remnants of a veil on the stalk of some mushrooms.

saprophytic: feeding on dead organic matter.

scabers: short projecting scales on stalk.

scales: pieces of tissue on the cap or stalk.

scaly: furnished with scales.

serrate: (of gills), notched or toothed on the edge.

species: an organism distinct from others by being unable to interbreed naturally with them.

specimen: an individual organism.

spore: the reproductive cell of a fungus.

spore case: the large chamber that holds the spores in puffballs and earthstars.

striate: (of caps), marked with fine lines or furrows.

substrate: the substance on or in which a fungus grows.

symbiosis: interdependence between different organisms.

terrestrial: growing on the ground.

toadstool: a derogatory term for mushroom.

tomentose: densely matted with a covering of soft hairs.

transluscent-striate: (of caps), gills show through as lines.

truffles: underground fruiting bodies.

umbo: a central knob on the cap.

umbonate: featuring an umbo.

variant: a deviation from the usual.

veil: tissue that covers and protects the immature gills or tubes of some mushrooms.

viscid: sticky to slimy when moist, sometimes shiny when dry.

volva: a sac-like cup or tissue on certain mushrooms surrounding the base of the stalk; remains of the fungal egg; Latin for womb.

zoned: (of the cap), marked with concentric bands.

Index

Boldface indicates mushroom species with descriptions and photographs.